Eileen Ford

Eileen Ford's
Book of Model
Beauty *Illustrated by Erica Merkling*

SIMON AND SCHUSTER   NEW YORK

I wish to thank Andrew Ettinger, who really pushed me into finishing this book. To Joan Rattner, Barbara Huntley, Mary Stanyan, Dr. Thomas Rees, Dr. Norman Orentreich, Dr. Marvin Stevens, Dr. Mary McCann and Dr. Fredrick Stare, Harvard School of Public Health, my undying gratitude for their invaluable counsel and time, without which I never could have written this book.

SBN 671-22260-0
Library of Congress Catalog Card Number: 67-28140
Manufactured in the United States of America

Thirteenth Printing

To my models, because I love them.
To my husband and partner—without him there's no me.

Contents

1
Introduction

Mother was a model, the first Best and Co. ever hired. I was a model, too, for a short time during my college days. Soon after, in 1946, my husband Jerry and I set up a model agency in New York, and we've been directing the working lives of about one hundred girls at a time ever since. Naturally, models come and go—eventually they move away, get married and have babies, or outgrow their profession—but the ones who leave are replaced by a stream of newcomers, all eager for success. So we've mothered, managed, guided, and nurtured over two thousand girls since we've gone into business.

Some of our girls were born beautiful. Others *learned* how to be beautiful. In fact, some of those who were not "perfect" turned out to be the most attractive and sought-after! And I've learned, working with them, probably all the beauty secrets there are to know. Each girl has had her own specific problem areas, her own personal assets, and together we discovered how to bring out the good and play down the bad.

The most interesting thing we found out in the agency is that even the least likely candidate for a model can often be groomed into a great beauty. I've come to believe that every woman can be beautiful—in her own way, perhaps—but beautiful. Everyone has tremendous potential— the trick is to develop it.

We've created the most successful fashion models from quite raw material. We've played Pygmalion with girls you'd never believe could make it—and I could prove it by showing you the dollars-and-cents records of their success.

Of course, I have learned how to recognize possible beauties at a glance—in fact, I discover some of our top talent walking down the street. But any woman can play Pygmalion with herself—I'm going to show her how in this book. The information we'll pass on to you is distilled from all those years of working with beauties. You'll find—as our girls have— that it can change your life. It can produce a success story for any woman, model or not. The results may be more striking, the example more startling with a model—after all, models do exaggerate for effect— but the woman who would never dream of such a career can apply exactly the same principles to herself and then watch her go! Her new confidence and assurance, the startling effect her changed appearance and poise have on others, can turn a drab life into an exciting one. I've seen it happen.

I met a girl one day when I was commentator at a fashion show in a large Midwest department store. She wasn't as young as her teen-age

2

clothes might indicate—she was about twenty-three. She was a stock clerk in the store. As I was talking to the large group of women, I spotted her: a tall, rangy girl with rather straggly shoulder-length hair, her only makeup a blob of lipstick slapped on a rather generous mouth. But she was a photographer's dream of facial planes and bone structure.

I couldn't resist the challenge. After the show, I went up to her quickly before she could escape. "Let me make you up?" I asked her. She laughed nervously, and agreed. When I finished, there was an entirely new face, a new blend of features, presenting all the beauty I'd spotted behind that drab exterior. We were both rather awed. She thanked me and left, looking not only beautiful but excited and with a tiny bit of added dignity.

Months passed and she slipped from my mind. Then I revisited the store and met her again—in fact, she came especially to see me. Her makeup was skillfully applied. She had discovered hairstyling. She walked with a new grace. She had a new and much better job. The former clerk, in fact, now had charge of a whole chorus of clerks. She could have been a model, but that wasn't for her. She wanted to fulfill her ambitions right there in the store—and it looked as though she were going to make it.

On one of my lecture tours, I met a handsome mature woman whose life I do believe changed with a few strokes of a pencil. She came up to speak to me after the talk. She wore simple, nondescript clothes though her figure was almost perfectly proportioned. Her hair was neatly coiffed —too neatly. She wore only a trace of lipstick and powder. Her brows and lashes were nearly colorless. She wanted my advice on improving her appearance.

"You need color," I said. "You especially need eye makeup, a lot of it."

"But I wear glasses," she protested.

"Certainly, you wear glasses," I replied. "But we can still see your eyes very clearly." I sat her down and within a few minutes I etched on new eyebrows and showed her how to use eye shadow and mascara—discreetly. I demonstrated how to wield a lip liner and talked about

3

foundation blends. It was a thrill even for an old hand like me to see her expression when she looked in the mirror.

A month later, she wrote me a letter. Her "new" eyes not only had added dramatically to her whole appearance but through them she had seen the need for color and contrast in her complete makeup and clothes as well. Her life became, literally, a more colorful one. She now felt a confidence quite new to her.

Exaggerated? Not at all. It was something that could happen any day—to you or any other woman. Beauty is there for the asking and doing, even when the problems are major. Not everyone can be a model, but there is not one woman who could not enhance her life by becoming just as attractive as possible. Such beauty, and the self-assurance that goes with it, affect you, your family, friends, fellow workers, even the people casually encountered.

It is never too late to start—the teen-ager who has let nature take too much of a course, the matron who has never tried (or has stopped trying) to make something of herself, or those in the later years who never took the time (or never knew how) —all of them can learn to reach their own kind of perfection.

No good ever came from resigning oneself to small colorless eyes, limp hair, bad skin, a lumpy, dumpy figure. Great good, however, can be done from facing the fact that you have such problems, and solving them.

I could write six books telling how specific successful models made the grade, but, just for encouragement, I'll tell you about one of our most famous girls.

A few years back, the top model in the whole of New York's fashion world—and, therefore, in the entire world—was Jean Patchett. Jean walked into our agency one day in 1949. She was fairly pretty, quite plump, and exceedingly dowdy. She wore an absurd little hat with a wispy veil perched on top of her long, flying schoolgirl hair. She weighed 135 pounds . . . much too much for her future career. She was five feet nine inches tall. Her rather nondescript suit was decorated by a set of jewelry—earrings, bracelet, necklace, and besides that, a lapel pin. I

4

looked at her and thought, "This girl has good potential but what a long way she has to go. Hair much too long and wild, the walk too awkward, too much waistline, eyebrows undisciplined, a mouth too petulant . . ."

But Jean was willing to work—just as you should—and she became a face every woman knew and admired.

N., however, was an example of a real beauty who needed just one truly major improvement, one that called for specialized assistance. N.'s is a face you've seen in every magazine, but when she came to the agency, she had the same great dark eyes, beautiful generous eyebrows, and heavy lashes—*and* a moustache! She had tried to hide it over the years and finally had just accepted it, believing her own and her family's fable that it "really didn't show." She said she couldn't afford the necessary professional treatment to get rid of her disfiguring superfluous hair.

She afforded it though. She didn't buy that fall coat she simply had to have—she went to a competent doctor instead. And the face you've been seeing is far prettier and far happier.

Now a full-length case history of one of our models. It will give you an idea of how you, too, can reach your own potential. After that, we'll work on a beauty program for *you*.

2

The Case History of a Model

I interview about three thousand models yearly, and I must see almost twenty tons of excess avoirdupois annually. The average would-be model weighs about sixteen pounds more than she should. When nineteen-year-old M. walked into our office a couple of months ago, she was carrying twenty-one such excess pounds on her five-foot, eight-inch frame.

Dreaming of a career as a model, lacking the confidence to try, M. worked as a waitress. But one day, encouraged by a chance encounter with a photographer, she climbed the stairs to our model agency, hesitantly turned the knob, and walked in.

Our newest hopeful had good basis for her hopes. M. did, indeed, have the frame, the bone structure, the height, and the features that could make her a good model. However, there was work to be done. Her hair hung shapelessly around her shoulders; she wore not a bit of makeup. She also had those twenty-one excess pounds!

The first thing to be done with a girl with a good potential is to make a detailed, ruthless, frank figure analysis complete with scales and measurements. M. weighed 137 pounds, and measured 36-inch bust, 26-inch waist, and 38½-inch hips. These figures were a far cry from the model's ideal measurements: 116 pounds, 34-inch bust, 22-inch waist, 34-inch hips.

We knew that a diet would reduce her weight, and that proper diet would be the secret of maintaining that weight. But what few girls seem to realize is that figure control is not just a matter of weight. Too many slender people have figure problems for this to be the case. The sad fact facing M. was: she could never really obtain the muscle tone essential to a good figure unless she exercised along with her diet.

I could have put together hundreds of different combinations of foods that effectively would have taken off whatever amount of weight M. had wished to lose, but these diets alone would never rid her—or anyone—of a bulging tummy, dowager's hump, flabby thighs, or any one of the many figure faults that plague us all.

I told M. that ten minutes of exercise a day, combined with proper diet, would give and keep for her the figure she sought. But, the ten minutes a day had to be as much a part of her daily routine as brushing her teeth, and the proper diet and exercise (once the excess weight was lost) had to be *a way of life.*

The time that a diet, exercise, and a beauty plan take to achieve 7 good results varies, of course, with the individual and her problems. It can't be speeded up to achieve quickie results—there is no shortcut to

true beauty. While she was on a well-balanced, nutritious, but low-calorie diet, M. had to plan to exercise daily.

To flatten her tummy, we used a combination of exercises. But the one she still uses to keep in shape is this one: lying on your back, lift legs together slowly in the air, then slowly let them down without touching the floor. Repeat this ten times daily.

To attack M.'s overlarge waistline, we again combined several exercises. The one she liked best is this: lie on side, extend arm in front of you and rest head on it. With legs pressed together, lift them up to the side and lower them rhythmically. Work up to ten times on each side.

Her pet hate was the thigh exercises, but she did them and still does. This is her standby: go into deep knee bend, hands on hips. Extend left leg forward and raise one or two inches from the floor, return. Then extend the right leg. Do this in rhythm and work up to ten times daily.

We started with only five minutes of exercise a day in order not to strain muscles used to long hours of inactivity. After a week or two, M. was able to exercise a full ten minutes every day, and from then on the change in her proportions was spectacular. Her hips and thighs, which had become soft through years of sitting at a school desk, began to resume their natural youthful firmness. Her waist lost the roll of fat, which had developed from sheer lack of muscle tone. As the flesh firmed, the inches melted away, and the path to the model's figure became clear.

While M. was perfecting her figure, she came to our office every other day for lessons in the techniques of makeup. Then, on the in-between days, she studied and practiced what we taught her.

The first makeup tool we worked with was foundation, because it

offers all of us excellent opportunities for improving the facial bone structure that God granted us. For instance, a too-round face can be slimmed to a near oval by carefully applying a darker base over the lighter base used as a general covering, in the area of the face where hollows should appear. This same principle can be used to shadow a too-square jaw or too-broad nose.

The principle to remember when using darker and lighter bases is that light protrudes and dark recedes. Therefore, whatever must be emphasized is treated with light makeup, whatever should appear less prominent is shaded with darker.

In the first makeup session, M. was told that makeup starts from the bare, freshly cleaned skin. As M.'s skin was clear, we had no blemish problems, praise be, for that can take weeks to correct. However, her skin does tend to be faintly sallow. We mixed both ivory- and beige-tinted liquid makeup together in one-to-three proportions to find exactly the shade of base that would lighten yet appear to blend naturally with M.'s skin tone.

We then used the pure beige-tone base to emphasize the hollows, as they began to appear below her cheekbones. We also used the pure beige base to shadow the sides of M.'s nose and a thin line of white makeup down the center to make it appear to the camera a fraction narrower than it really is. Then home she went to practice, practice, practice, to master the application of her base to such perfection that it looked like her own skin.

Having learned to apply her base properly, M. was then ready for our analysis of her eyes. We had to find the most effective way of shaping them into dramatic, larger-than-large, wide-set eyes. This meant that I

9

had to draw many sets of lines on her eyes until we found the magic combination. The first step in perfecting her eye makeup was the tweezing of her unplucked brows. The shape was basically good, but we had to remove all the stray hairs that prevented her from having a tidy appearance.

Step two was to apply white eye shadow beneath M.'s lovely brown eyes, this to mask a slight shadowing there. This white had to be carefully blended to avoid a clownlike appearance. Next, we applied pale green eye shadow over her top eyelid, followed by a black eyeline along the upper lid. This line was carefully extended out, and we then drew a faint line of gray under the lower lashes, extending a bit to form a triangle with this black line. The center of the triangle was filled with white pencil, thus lengthening her eye considerably.

Next we added false eyelashes, which I had cut and shaped with a razor blade, to M.'s eyelids. False eyelashes are exciting eye dramatics. It takes a while to trim them properly to fit anyone's eyes, however, and then several hours more before the eyes become accustomed to them. A razor blade is used to trim each lash until finally every hair blends naturally with those on the eyelid. Then they must be carefully applied to the place from which the real eyelashes grow, just on top of the real ones, fastened there with a thin line of surgical adhesive.

Finally, I drew on her eyebrows in tiny, tiny strokes with a dark-brown eyebrow pencil that matched her own brows, arching them ever so slightly to raise them a bit from the eye. Again she had to practice by the hour, learning how to use the pencils, brushes, and shadow deftly and quickly. She had to learn how to shape and draw her eyebrows into the exact arch we had decided would be her perfect eye frame.

Finally, M. had become a consummate artist in making her eyes absolutely right from every camera angle. Draw, erase, draw, erase—patience and self-analysis are what one needs to achieve the perfect eye makeup techniques.

10

Having worked out M.'s best eye makeup combinations, we turned our attention to the most commonly used and misused cosmetic—that old standby, lipstick. M. had a good, but not perfect, mouth. It was a

trifle small. Happily this is the easiest feature to correct. We studied her mouth without lipstick for size and shape.

A small mouth must be lengthened by carefully building up the upper lip at the center and extending it a bit above the natural lip line to the corners, using a good lip liner, one of the most essential tools of any model's trade; then the lower lip often has to be enlarged slightly to compensate for this increase in size.

I have never found a tape measure by which to measure a beautiful mouth precisely, but we worked toward finding a shape that was in harmony with the overall proportion of M.'s face; and this is the point at which a model's makeup technique can become makeup art. We powdered her lips first to prevent smearing or the formation of small vertical lines, then we applied the lip liner, then filled in with lipstick.

M.'s coiffure was one of the last points to be settled. For, just as you choose a hat after you've selected a costume, so must a coiffure be chosen to fit the person who emerges from a beauty program.

Everyone is always ready to accept my advice on makeup and diet. But for reasons that probably date back to prehistoric times, most women guard their hair as if their very lives depended on it. M.'s lovely shoulder-length brown hair had to be cut in five separate sittings, and she howled every inch of the way!

11

Why girls treasure each lock I don't know. I do know that to be a Ford model, however, a girl must have hair that does not touch her shoulders, and is "convertible." It must lend itself to dozens of different photographic situations.

For M., we decided to have her hair cut blunt, or even, all the way around, about two inches below her ears. This hairdo made it possible for her to wear her hair in many ways, depending on the demands of the photographic situation.

This, too, takes an investment of time on the part of the would-be model. She must learn how to "convert" her hair herself. M. worked with a hairdresser for many weeks before she mastered the tricks of teasing and rearranging her hair into the styles that would be demanded of her.

After two months of intensive work, our model-to-be was ready. She had mastered her makeup and hair, she had slimmed by diet and exercise to perfect measurements, she had learned the myriad details that go with good grooming. And she had made the philosophy of each a part of her everyday thinking. She truly "walks proud" and "thinks beautiful," as a successful model or any really attractive woman must.

Many days of devoted attention to this new career have passed since M. walked up the stairs to The Fords. From a merely pretty girl, she has turned into a girl who is not only beautiful but also poised and confident. Now her apprenticeship is finished, and she's ready to set out to see if she'll become one of the big names in the fashion world.

Not everyone can or wants to become a model, but the short course in beauty that M. has just completed can help everyone reach her own beauty potential.

Use the secrets I've told you about her and see what they'll do for you!

3
How to Take
Your True Measure

The first step in becoming a beauty is to make a plan. Then you must stick to it as if your very life depended on it. Better looks, better health, and greater poise never came from a hit-and-miss series of experiments with cosmetics, diet, and exercise. Your plan will take time, and you must be conscientious. It won't require a lot of time out of your

day, but it must be every day, like brushing your teeth. You'll soon learn to fit it easily into your life.

Start with an honest and thorough consultation with your mirror. Resolve to be as ruthless as I would be if you were a prospective model whom I was determined to transform into a cover girl. Check off, feature by feature, measure by measure, what is wrong and what is right.

At The Fords we start with a girl's figure. So let's start there with you.

Strip down to panties and bra, or better still, just strip down. Arm yourself with a tape measure and your true, up-to-the-minute weight.

Now measure. Compare your results with my Desirable Proportions and Desirable Weights charts. It may be a shocking revelation and, if that's so, the shock will be a treatment in itself. This is the moment of decision—and you may be grateful the rest of your life! Your chin line, upper arms, thighs, and legs may need trimming down or building up. You may have an under- or oversized bust, hips, and waist. Make a checklist of the areas that need changing. And don't be discouraged—you are not alone, and *it can be done.*

Keep in mind this book with its advice on nutrition, diet, posture, poise, and exercise, plus the calorie chart you'll find in the nutrition chapter. It won't be long before you'll see remarkable changes. You must learn your lessons well—and learn them for life.

Next, like the girl motivated by the lure of the photographers' lights, you must devote a session to your face. You'll need your dressing-table mirror as well as a good magnifying hand-mirror—and very bright candid lights. Wear your glasses for part of this self-analysis if necessary. Just be sure they're not rose colored!

Ask yourself these questions: is my complexion clear? Am I withering on the vine or erupting anywhere? Is my skin dry or oily? Do I have dark shadows anywhere on my face? What shape is my face? Is my chin too small or too strong? Are my eyes large, small, far apart, close set? Are my eyebrows right for my eyes? Too thick? Too thin? Is there superfluous hair on my face? What about my mouth—does it need reshaping? Could my hair be improved by styling, tinting, or a new hairline? Do I need to learn about special treatments and shampoos to give it life and body?

At the very end of your self-analysis, consider the rest of you. Are your hands smooth and soft? Your legs properly de-fuzzed? Are you meticulous in your removal of underarm hair? How about your feet and elbows? What shape are they in?

Nothing sets the facts so firmly in mind as writing them down. Here is a checklist. Note each area to be examined, fill in your own personal description, measurements, problems to be dealt with. Be sure to write down every detail.

Under comments, write what you think needs special attention. Most of your problems, you'll find, can be coped with yourself—with a little help.

Are you sure you've examined yourself completely, head to toe? Do you know all the areas that need improvement, those that should be emphasized, those to be played down? When the ruthless examination is finished, you are ready to start your beauty program. The top experts in the field agree that the following table of heights and weights is a standard guide to the best (that is, healthiest) weights for women at age twenty-five and over. Because people come in a variety of sizes and shapes, large-boned or small-boned, firm-muscled or flaccid, short and stocky, or tall and lanky, and many variations in between, no one weight is right for everyone of the same height, age, or sex. The weight that is best for you depends upon your individual framework, muscular development, and height. It is usually the weight at which you look and feel your best.

In our business, of course, the weight problem is much more crucial. Just a few pounds in the wrong place can ruin a modeling assignment, a very expensive advertising illustration—or a career!

Please note, too, that the weights listed include indoor clothing and shoes. The heights allow for shoes with two-inch heels. If you usually weigh yourself on the bathroom scale without shoes, and perhaps without any clothing, these factors must be taken into account and adjustments made before you find your desirable weight. For nude weights, subtract two to four pounds.

DESIRABLE WEIGHTS
(In indoor clothing—compiled by the Metropolitan Life Insurance Co.)

	HEIGHT (shoes on)	SMALL FRAME	MEDIUM FRAME	LARGE FRAME
	4′10″	92–98	96–107	104–119
	4′11″	94–101	98–110	106–122
	5′0″	96–104	101–113	109–125
Women	5′1″	99–107	104–116	112–128
of Ages 25*	5′2″	102–110	107–119	115–131
and Over	5′3″	105–113	110–122	118–134
	5′4″	108–116	113–126	121–138
	5′5″	111–119	116–130	125–142
	5′6″	114–123	120–135	129–146
	5′7″	118–127	124–139	133–150
	5′8″	122–131	128–143	137–154
	5′9″	126–135	132–147	141–158
	5′10″	130–140	136–151	145–163
	5′11″	134–144	140–155	149–168
	6′0″	138–148	144–159	153–173

* For girls between 18 and 25, subtract 1 pound for each year under 25.

DESIRABLE PROPORTIONS FOR WOMEN
(According to me, Eileen Ford)

HEIGHT 4′10″ to 5′
Bust: 30 to 31
Waist: 19 to 20
Hips: 31 to 32

HEIGHT 5′1″ to 5′4″
Bust: 32
Waist: 20 to 21
Hips: 33

HEIGHT 5′5″ to 5′7″
Bust: 33
Waist: 21 to 23
Hips: 33

HEIGHT 5′8″
Bust: 34
Waist: 23 to 24
Hips: 34 to 35

HEIGHT 5′9″ to 6′
Bust: 35 to 37
Waist: 25 to 26
Hips: 35 to 37

17

BEAUTY CHECKLIST

Present condition	2 weeks	3 weeks	4 weeks
WEIGHT:			
MEASUREMENTS:			
Bust			
Arms (Upper)			
Waist			
Hips			
Thighs			
Calves			
HAIR:			
SKIN:			
Face			
Neck			
Body			
FACIAL SHAPE:			
MAKEUP:			
GROOMING:			
POSTURE:			

18

BEAUTY CHECKLIST

5 weeks	6 weeks	Comments

Monday
Tuesday
Wednesday
Thursday
...day
...urday
...ay

4
The Beauty Program

"Who is that attractive woman?" You? It will be if you're willing to set off on my beauty plan. It will cost a little money and a lot of time—at first. Once you've mastered the plan, you'll find you can cut down drastically on both. The hour or so a day you'll need at the start will be cut to half that time once you're "trained." And that is precious little to give for such rich rewards. Even if you are the busy mother of four children (as I am), a woman who combines a business career with home-making (as I do), is that too much time to spend on yourself? Don't you usually take that much time every day for a television program, a maga-zine story, a gossip session on the telephone? My most successful models never neglect themselves for a day—they can't afford to—and they lead the busiest lives of any girls in town. You'll soon see that it does pay off. Just make up your mind to find the time. Everyone can.

1. Exercise (we'll give you the details later). You'll need about ten minutes a day for this—for posture and grace, for a companion to diet, or to reduce a special area of your body. Most of our models prefer taking five minutes of exercise first thing in the morning, and another five minutes at bedtime. I've found the eleven o'clock news a good time to absorb information while I do mine. Some women prefer ten minutes all at one time, perhaps in midmorning. Just do it when you are completely comfortable, unencumbered by many clothes, girdles, or carefully combed hairdos.

When you make your decision, write the time down on your beauty program. If nine A.M. is your time for exercise, it's harder to skip than if you just hope to fit it in whenever the mood strikes you.

21

2. Face cleansing. There are no exceptions to the rule that cleansing must be among the first things done in the morning, along with brushing your teeth. Clean your face carefully, following the method you'll find in this book.

3. Makeup. The timing for this depends on your own way of life. Housewives often prefer to tie a kerchief about their heads, put on a swift bit of lipstick, and leave the serious business until later when they're about to go out. But the girls who are due at a desk must take care of this job immediately. First foundation, eye makeup, and hairdo. Lipstick should wait till after breakfast. Brush and comb your hair into place. I can't honestly predict how long this will take *you;* everyone works at a different rate and some people are more deft than others. But please believe that, once the skills are acquired, fifteen minutes is not too little time to plan on. While you're learning, you'll need more time for perhaps a month.

For a while, you'll need to apportion another fifteen minutes or so to makeup lessons. If you're home, take them right after your coffee. Career girls often find that after dinner is a good time for leisurely practice. Trial and error—that's the only way you'll discover just what makeup tricks work best for you.

4. Beauty stretch. This is a boon that you should make every effort to fit into your day. It will take about ten minutes. Lie down on the floor or bed, prop your feet up about twelve inches higher than your head, close your eyes, and relax. Try to "float." Don't go to sleep!

5. Nighttime ritual. Whatever your daily activities, you must do a good job on yourself before you go to bed—remove makeup and give your face a thorough cleansing, before proceeding with stimulating and lubricating.

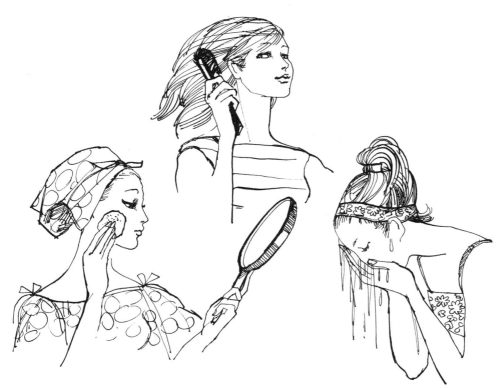

6. Coiffure. When you set your hair is up to you, but remember that there are few hairdos that do not need daily care and "pinning up." Fit it into your day, either in the morning while you do your housework, or at night. But please don't go out of the house wearing a headful of rollers—this is private business. Whatever time you choose, allow another two or three minutes for a good brushing.

These are the basic chores. Then there is a short list of once-a-week beauty jobs.

I recommend assigning one job each weekday, leaving the weekend free. That's why I suggest this schedule for you to rearrange as it suits you:

Monday: pedicure and reset hair if needed.
Tuesday: manicure.
Wednesday: depilatory or shaving legs, arms, underarms.
Thursday: eyebrow and hairline grooming, manicure touch-up.
Friday: shampoo and set.

Of course, you can do all of this at once, if you find that works out best for you. And try to do a little additional homework: read books on

23

nutrition, study the fashion magazines, go to a fashion show, along with practicing your beauty techniques.

Remember that, when we start to work with prospective models at The Fords, they aren't models either. They are simply hopeful—and the future successful ones are willing to make an effort. Their goal may be different from yours, but the principles are identical. You have a debt to yourself—you must try to become the most attractive woman you can possibly be. I had an invitation recently to speak to the women's group of New York City's American Institute of Finance. There was a record turnout and the interest was memorable. "But why," I asked the officials, "are you so interested that your employees—all of whom work for banks—hear about beauty fulfillment?"

They had a most practical, bankerlike response. They've learned that a woman who looks her best has the confidence to do good work. If she works constantly toward improving herself personally, she is more likely to work well at her job. And she inspires confidence in the people with whom she deals. Besides, anyone who is the representative of a firm must project its image attractively.

Here is a sample beauty program. It's suited for a busy gal, so vary it to fit yourself, but stick to it until it becomes part of your life.

BEAUTY PROGRAM FOR

Mornings

Monday through Friday:

    7:00–7:05—Exercise.

    7:05–7:10—Shower, cleanse face, rinse well. Apply deodorant, cologne, hand and body lotion moisturizer.

    7:10–7:30—Dress, all but outer garments. Apply foundation and eye makeup. Fix your hair.

    7:30–7:50—Have a good, calorie-counted breakfast.

    7:50–8:00—Put on outer garments. Apply lipstick.

Noons

After calorie-counted lunch, try to relax for ten minutes—feet up. Tidy face and hair. Reapply lipstick.

Evenings

Calorie-counted dinner.

Then:

MONDAY: Pedicure. Practice applying two shades of foundation on face. At bedtime, cleanse face, apply freshener and lubrication. Five minutes of exercise. Roll up hair for night.

TUESDAY: Manicure. Practice and experiment with hair styles. Same bedtime routine.

WEDNESDAY: Remove hair from legs, arms, underarms. Practice with lipstick and lip liner technique. Same bedtime routine. Check up on calorie program.

THURSDAY: Groom eyebrows and hairline. Practice eye makeup. Touch up manicure. Bedtime routine.

FRIDAY: Shampoo and set hair. Check figure measurements and weight. Bedtime routine.

Weekends

If you've been too busy during the week for these chores, do them now. Inspect your clothes for laundering, cleaning, mending. Do your reading.

Soon you won't need a schedule—you'll find you'll do everything quite automatically. It will be a real part of your life.

5
The Beautiful Part
of Diet

If you want to be a beauty, you have to be healthy. No matter how skillfully you apply makeup, what kind of hairdo you evolve, what shape your figure is in, you need that glow of health and well-being. Beauty really does come from the inside. The outside is extra. Many prospective models come to my office, perhaps pretty and well groomed, yet with that lackluster look of fatigue and droop. Their complexions look tired, their hair limp, their nails are brittle, and they often look just plain hungry—some of them starve themselves to reduce to what they think is model size.

I am not a doctor, and I can't discuss serious health problems—if you have a chronic ailment or a deficiency, you must go to your doctor and start treatment immediately. But many women have nothing the matter with them except an advanced case of personal neglect of healthy living habits. In their frenzy to lose weight, many don't eat the foods necessary for their well-being. It is quite possible to reduce or to remain thin without jeopardizing your health—remember there are certain foods that everyone must have every day, diet or no diet. You'll find my Ford Diet (read on!) will keep you in shape without such problems.

To have that glow of health, you must get enough sleep. Most people seem to need from six to eight hours every night to be in top form; you'll have to decide this for yourself. Consistent lack of sleep may cause your skin to lose its tone and color, make your hair lack luster, give you dull eyes and dark circles, besides an air of "it's all too much."

Too much drinking and smoking will contribute their toll to your looks, too. Try to keep both in moderation or cut them out altogether. And keep in mind that sweet breath is part of the beauty picture—big drinkers and smokers seldom have that.

Your body tone must be in good condition, and that's where exercises play an important part. Flab is not part of the picture we want to paint. If your stomach sticks out or your back humps over, you will not be a beauty, no matter what.

Of all the health factors, perhaps what you eat (or don't eat) is the most important to your appearance. It certainly is the one that women talk about the most. Listen to a group of women for just one evening, and I'll bet at least one of them will mention "going on a diet." She's overweight—or maybe underweight—and she *must* do something about it. She'll start "tomorrow."

But what kind of diet? I have heard unbelievable tales of the eating habits of supposedly intelligent women. Some are guaranteed to wreck the health—I remember the story of a girl from Philadelphia who wanted desperately to be a model. She almost died of malnutrition while on a diet of shrimp and black coffee, and she not only did *not* become a Ford model, she spent long months convalescing in a hospital. Remember the famous American heiress who irreparably damaged her entire digestive system by starving herself periodically? Even if you don't do anything so extreme, you can make yourself (and your family) miserable if you don't go about dieting sensibly. You can't stick with fad diets for very long, they get so dull and boring. Eventually you'll go off on a spree, eating wildly to compensate for everything you've been missing. No one can live happily very long on a banana diet, a peanut diet, a lettuce diet, or one of those liquid diet plans. And even if you manage to lose weight, you'll gain it all back once you've quit if you don't watch yourself carefully.

The proper kind of diet gives you all the nutrition your body needs, it doesn't leave you ravenously hungry, it gives you enough variety so that you don't feel the need of a spree. What you must keep in mind is that proper eating habits can't be a thing of the moment—or even a few months—they must become a way of life for you.

Now, just what makes us fat? Under-activity and overeating. If we take in more calories than we use, we gain weight. The source of excess calories doesn't matter—carbohydrates, fats, protein, or alcohol. If we don't burn them up in our day's activities, these calories are stored in the body as fat. If we take in 4500 calories a day in food and use only 1000, there are 3500 extra calories for the body to store—and 3500 extra calories will make about one pound of extra body fat! Even if you take in the extra 3500 over a week or a year—it means another pound.

Let's think of putting what we eat on a scale. We have taken in, let's say, 2000 calories that day. Put them on one side of the scale. On the other side, the number of calories we've burned, is say 1500. With such a calorie imbalance, we will gain weight! If we use up more than the 2000, we will lose weight!

Suppose you are five feet five inches tall, with a desirable weight of 125 pounds. You need roughly 2250 calories daily to maintain that weight, if you are moderately active. To lose weight, you must take in fewer than the 2250. If you cut 1000 calories from this daily intake, you will lose about two pounds a week.

To find out how many calories you use, take the midpoint of the desirable weight range for your height. Multiply this figure by eighteen (twenty-one for a man). The answer will be the approximate number of calories used daily by a moderately active adult.

To check your intake of calories consult the complete list of foods at the end of this book.

Here is a chart* giving rough estimates of the calories expended in various activities. Obviously, if you are very active, your body burns up more calories.

CALORIE EXPENDITURES

Type of Activity:

	CALORIES PER HOUR
SEDENTARY ACTIVITIES, such as reading; writing; eating; watching television or movies; listening to the radio; sewing; playing cards; and typing, miscellaneous office work, and other activities done while sitting that require little or no arm movement.	80 to 100

* U.S. Department of Agriculture.

29

LIGHT ACTIVITIES, such as preparing and cooking food; doing dishes; dusting; handwashing small articles of clothing; ironing; walking slowly; personal care; miscellaneous office work and other activities done while standing that require some arm movement; and rapid typing and other activities done while sitting that are more strenuous.   110 to 160

MODERATE ACTIVITIES, such as making beds; mopping and scrubbing; sweeping; light polishing and waxing; laundering by machine; light gardening and carpentry work; walking moderately fast; other activities done while standing that require moderate arm movement; and activities done while sitting that require more vigorous arm movement.   170 to 240

VIGOROUS ACTIVITIES, such as heavy scrubbing and waxing; hand washing large articles of clothing; hanging out clothes; stripping beds; other heavy work; walking fast; bowling; golfing; and gardening.   250 to 350

30

STRENUOUS ACTIVITIES, such as swimming; playing tennis; running; bicycling; dancing; skiing; and playing football.

350 and more

As a former "fatty" myself, I know how hard it is to follow any advice about food. And I've seen the problems our models have had in getting and staying in shape. The five following rules I've devised to make the process as painless as possible. Study them, stick to them, make them your own. The results will be spectacular.

1. *Shop thin* by buying only the leanest cuts of meat, the freshest fruits, fish, poultry, and vegetables. Skip the tempting goodies—there's lots to be said of that old adage, "out of sight, out of mind," so buy only what is on your diet. If you don't have blueberry pie, coffee cake, soft drinks, or ice cream in the house, you can't sneak into the kitchen for them.

2. *Drink thin* by drinking your liquids *between* meals, rather than *with* them. And stick to water, skimmed milk, diet drinks, coffee, tea, rather than the more pound-happy types.

3. *Eat thin* by eating only what is on your diet. Eat small portions—and eat more frequently if you get hungry. There's no need to starve, but you must shrink your stomach to avoid hunger pangs. To help control your appetite, try eating a snack an hour before meals—but *only* Ford snacks. These are raw carrots, raw mushrooms, tomatoes, celery, watercress, raw cauliflower, lettuce, or a glass of skimmed milk.

4. *Cook thin* by broiling or roasting your meats and cooking vegetables quickly in a small amount of water and as little salt as possible. Discover the joys of cooking with herbs to make these old standby vegetables taste like gourmet dishes, rather than piling on the butter.

5. *Think thin.* This is the real model's trick. Tell yourself you really don't like rich foods, look askance at candy and say, "I never touch it." Look in the mirror every day and see how slim you're becoming. One girl at our agency used to be a chocolate-bar addict. You'd never see her without one and her skin and figure were beginning to show the effects. I convinced her to think thin—I admit it took a while—and she told me the other day that she hadn't touched a chocolate bar in over a year. "I just convinced myself I hated them." I doubt if you'll ever get to the point where you hate rich food, but at least you won't crave it.

I have made up a special Ford Model Diet for our models. Most of the girls who come to us are overweight. For everyday life, they're about six to eight pounds overweight, and for modeling, they carry about twelve to sixteen pounds of excess fat (the camera adds poundage). If they want to work for us, they must lose. They *do* on our diet—and you can, too. You'll lose gradually until you have the optimum number of pounds for your height.

Hundreds of our girls have followed the Ford Model Diet with good results. It's simple, it allows for lots of variety, and you won't find yourself aching for extras. It contains all the essential daily requirements for good nutrition. It also includes between-meal snacks. You'll find that you can eat quite normally, sitting at the table with your family and not spoiling mealtime for yourself or the others. You'll lose weight but you'll gain in energy and a feeling of well-being.

Here it is:

FORD MODEL DIET

BREAKFAST: Grapefruit juice, half grapefruit, half cantaloupe, or orange juice. One or two boiled or poached eggs. Black coffee, with sugar substitute.

MIDMORNING: One or two raw carrots, celery stalks, raw mushrooms, tomatoes, watercress, raw cauliflower, lettuce.

LUNCH: Broiled hamburger or two hard-boiled eggs. Raw tomato and raw carrots. (I suggest you use a pepper mill for seasoning to cut down on salt.)

COCKTAIL TIME: One cup bouillon, raw snacks.

DINNER: Tomato, vegetable or grapefruit juice, or tomato soup. Broiled steak, liver, lamb chop, chicken, fish, hamburger, or roast lamb, beef, or chicken. Spinach, string beans, tomatoes, carrots, cabbage, or broccoli (no butter). Salad with lemon juice and fresh pepper dressing, or wine-garlic vinegar and light oil. Half grapefruit, medium slice of watermelon, or half cantaloupe. Coffee.

If you are underweight, you must do the opposite of the fatty. Those of us who have the tendency to gain are always envious of you, but I know your problem can be just as distressing. If you are strikingly underweight for no apparent cause, do be certain to see a competent doctor before you do another thing. There may be a medical reason for your situation. But, generally speaking, the principle of gaining is

33

exactly the same as it is for the rest of us: it's the calorie intake and output that counts. To gain weight you decrease activity and increase calorie intake. Do just the opposite to lose. Simple as that.

One excellent way to add 900 extra calories to your daily food intake is to drink one glass of a 300-calorie drink about ten A.M.; another about two P.M.; and a third before you go to bed. Eat normally at mealtimes. Never skip meals or have just a snack instead. You know all the more fattening foods—you've certainly heard your friends talk about avoiding them! Stow these away as much as you can—but never before meals so they'll ruin your appetite.

Chances are the underweight girl doesn't get as much rest as she should. Exercise is vital for everyone, but remember that your body burns up more calories when you are active. Try to get as much sleep at night as possible. And have an afternoon nap if you can manage it.

Overweight or underweight, to maintain the size you've achieved, you have to continue good eating habits. If you've lost weight, you'll need fewer calories each day to maintain your present size. If you've gained, you'll need more. On a *permanent* basis. That's why I say diet must be a way of life—forever. Diets are not just for people with obvious problems—they're for *you,* always, if you want to look your best. If a model can do it, you can too. It won't be difficult once you've trained your appetite to know what to want. Eat, and as you eat, remember, you are eating your way to health and beauty.

6
Nutrition–
Your Inside Story

In case you've forgotten, since those long-ago days of home-economics courses, here is a rundown of the essential elements contained in the food you eat. To eat a balanced diet, you must have some of all of them.

1. Proteins. This is the stuff that keeps us going—every single cell in our bodies needs protein, an abundance of it that must be replaced daily because it cannot be stored. To determine the daily amount of protein adequate for you, take your weight, divide it in half—that is the approximate number of grams you need to keep healthy. For example, if you weigh 130 pounds, then your daily quota of protein would be about 65 grams.

Protein is contained in eggs, cheese, milk, poultry, meats, and fish. It also can be found in some vegetables such as peas and lima beans. Other sources are soybeans, cereals, and peanuts.

A deficiency in protein can result in all kinds of unpleasantness such as flabby muscles, sagging facial tissues, and all-round body deterioration.

2. Carbohydrates. These are the principal source of energy. If you don't eat enough, the body burns up the protein needed for tissue repair. If you consume more than the body needs, the excess turns into fat, stored away in the body. Carbohydrates are found in starches and sugars, such as breads, cereals, pastas, potatoes, rice, sweets like jellies, molasses, syrup, soft drinks. Others are found in fruits, juices, and of course just plain sugar and candy.

3. Fats. These provide energy too, and are the most concentrated source of calories. They help maintain the health of the skin, giving it a thin underlayer that acts as a cushion. You must include some fats in your diet every day, but I suggest you try to stick with the poly-unsaturated varieties—oils that include cottonseed, corn, soybean, and

peanut, and the oils of fish and seafood. The saturated fats, which are hard at room temperature, include—among others—butter, margarine, whole-milk cheese, solid shortenings, meat fats, and chocolate. It's best to stay away from these as much as possible.

4. Vitamins. Vital for overall health, vitamins are found in small quantities in many foods. The water-soluble vitamins are tricky things, and if you aren't careful, you can lose them through overcooking, too much cooking water, and the use of baking soda in cooking. Other vitamin losses occur by peeling fruits and vegetables, in the freezing and defrosting process, and by letting vegetables wilt. Some of the water-soluble vitamins in vegetables are extracted by the liquid present during cooking. Use the cooking water from vegetables in soups or vegetable cocktails. These are the vitamins you need:

Vitamin A. This lovely vitamin keeps your skin firm and glowing by nourishing the underlayer of fat directly beneath the skin. A deficiency can result in thin, dry hair, nails that crack and peel, night blindness, as well as many more serious health problems. The richest sources of Vitamin A are liver, whole milk, butter, eggs, and cheese made with whole milk. In addition, the carotene in some fresh vegetables changes to Vitamin A in the body, so you can be pretty sure of getting enough if you include bright green or yellow vegetables in your diet. Good sources of carotene include dark green leafy vegetables, carrots, papayas, apricots, and cantaloupe. Fortunately, Vitamin A is stored by the body for quite a while, so you needn't replenish your supply daily.

37

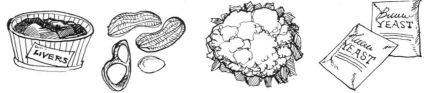

Vitamin B_1 (thiamine). If friends and family find you quarrelsome, uncooperative, tired and fearful, check on your B_1 intake. This is your joy-of-living vitamin, and with an adequate amount, the world should look rosy again. It whets your appetite, aids your nervous and digestive systems, and helps the body to use energy-producing carbohydrates. The richest sources are pork, organ meats (liver, heart, and kidneys), yeast, liver sausage, lean meats, eggs, green leafy vegetables, whole or enriched cereals, berries, nuts, and legumes.

Vitamin B_2 (riboflavin). This wondrous vitamin contributes much to health. Eyes are brighter and nerves are calmer with a sufficient intake. A deficiency can cause dermatitis, and with a real deficiency, fissures at the corner of the mouth, among other things. So you can see how important it is to get enough of this vitamin. Richest sources are milk, cheese, yogurt, leafy green vegetables, peas, soybeans, almonds, enriched grains, poultry, kidney, and liver.

Vitamin B_6 (pyridoxine). This is an elusive vitamin and must be supplied daily. It helps an oily skin, which is itself a cause of blackheads and skin problems. Richest sources are liver, meats, green vegetables, whole grain cereals and bread, egg yolks, milk, yeast, soybeans, and peanuts.

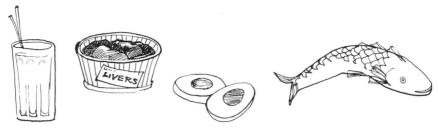

Vitamin B$_{12}$. This is said to be the most effective anti-anemic substance known per unit weight and is a lifesaver to those suffering from pernicious anemia. The animal foods are the best source for this vitamin, while the plant products are deficient in B$_{12}$. So, if you are on a vegetable diet, you may need a supplementary dose of it. Richest sources are organ meats, fish, milk, and yogurt.

Vitamin C (ascorbic acid). This is one of the best-known vitamins and is responsible for keeping us healthy in many ways. Your teeth and gums need it to be firm and healthy; it is an aid in preventing the breaking of surface capillaries that result in unsightly black-and-blue marks; it helps guard against infections. This, too, is an elusive vitamin and must be taken every day since it can't be stored. It is easily destroyed in cooking, so use the minimum amount of water and don't overcook. Baking soda, while it brings out the color of the vegetables, will also steal away the vitamins. Richest sources are citrus fruits, tomatoes, leafy green vegetables, green peppers, berries and melons, apples, and baked or boiled potatoes.

Vitamin D. This is known as the sunshine vitamin because your body manufactures it when exposed to the sun's rays. Soaking up sunshine is the best way to get D. You need it for good teeth and bones. The richest food sources are tuna, mackerel, salmon, herring, sardines, and milk fortified with Vitamin D.

Vitamin E. If you eat a normal diet, it's almost impossible to be deficient in E, but, just in case, the richest sources are corn, cottonseed oil, and wheat germ oil.

Vitamin K. As with Vitamin E, the body obligingly manufactures this vitamin, so with a normal diet you can hardly lack K.

Niacin. This is a stable vitamin, with little destruction occurring in cooking. It is the anti-pellagra vitamin and is prescribed for frayed nerves and diseases of the mouth and gums, among other things. Richest sources are liver, heart, lean meat, fish and poultry, peanuts and seeds, potatoes, most fruits and vegetables, yeast, whole grains and bread, and wheat germ.

5. Minerals. Somehow minerals don't seem nearly as fascinating as vitamins, but they are just as important.

Calcium. Needed for strong bones and teeth, healthy gums. It's found in milk, cottage cheese, yellow cheeses, yogurt, sesame seeds, broccoli, turnip greens.

40

Iron. Makes your lips red and gives a glow to your complexion besides pep to your step. It's the anti-anemia mineral and helps the vitamins do their good work. Richest sources are eggs, yeast, liver, lentils, soybeans, avocados, and oysters.

Phosphorous and fluoride help in the proper utilization of calcium and therefore promote good teeth and bones. If you get enough calcium in your milk intake, you also get enough phosphorus. Richest sources are eggs, milk, cottage cheese, yogurt, poultry, fish, lean meats. For fluoride one generally has to depend on fluoridated water. Fluoridation is one of the greatest advances of public health in this generation.

Iodine. To have a healthy thyroid gland, you must have sufficient iodine. The thyroid regulates your metabolism and therefore your weight and energy level. You usually get enough iodine in iodized table salt. Richest sources are iodized salt, sea fish, shellfish.

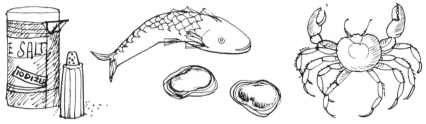

There are other minerals you must have, but they are usually quite sufficiently supplied in an ordinary diet.

A word about taking added vitamin and mineral concentrates: these pills or liquids will protect you against vitamin loss from overcooking, peeling, freezing, and storing foods and will provide nutrients at a time when you are unable, for some reason, to have a correct diet. However, no concentrate can take the place of nutritious foods, everyday foods, which remain the best sources of vitamins and minerals. If you take concentrates, don't overdo them—the body can absorb only certain amounts of vitamins and minerals and sometimes you can do yourself harm by thinking that if one pill does good, more will do better. It won't, and it might even be bad for you.

Keep track of what you eat for a week, writing down every bite. Then check to see if you've been skipping any of the vital elements of good nutrition. If you have all the basic nutritional elements in your diet, then you can start counting calories. If you start the other way around, you may end up as one of our models did—flat on your back in bed for a month.

41

7
Shaping Your Figure with Exercise

There's never been a Ford model yet who hasn't looked at me in despair when I've said (and I say it every day), "You'll have to exercise." "But why?" some of them ask. "I'm thin enough now." Then I explain that, in order to keep a figure, thin or not, in good shape, exercise is essential. It won't cause you to lose much weight, even if you need to lose, but it can change your dimensions. You can streamline your figure where it needs streamlining, or build it up where it needs building. Exercise keeps your muscles in good tone, and years from now—if you're young now—you'll be glad you didn't allow yourself to turn to flab. Exercise is the only thing, too, that can give you the balance, coordination, and ease of movement that are essential to beauty. And it stimulates circulation, keeps the complexion glowing, and eyes sparkling.

Now I know that, unless you are sports-minded or in training for the Olympics, the idea of daily exercise is probably horrendous. But, if it can do all those wonderful things for you, why fight it? Remember the figure you'll be saving is your own.

There must be millions of roads paved to nowhere with all the good intentions of all the girls who have started on an exercise regime, and then—after four or five days of enthusiasm—petered out to nothing. Most of us blame it on a lack of time, but is ten minutes a day so much to put to such a good purpose? Any exercise you do is good for you, but to do you the most good, you must do it *daily*. Pick the time of day that fits best into your schedule—before breakfast, right after breakfast, mid-morning, before bed. When will you be able to devote those ten whole minutes every single day without fail? Pick the time and then stick to it. Believe me when I say that, after years of experience with thousands of models, I know this is the way you must do it. If you decide just to fit in the exercise whenever the mood strikes you, you'll find—as they did—that the mood won't strike you many days, and soon the whole plan will go the way of many other good intentions. Exercise must be a habit if you don't want to end up looking like a lump.

It will pay off, I assure you. Not only will you soon be in fine trim, but it will be such fun to hear the comments: "Look at that girl's figure," or "Are you really the mother of a nineteen-year-old daughter—you have such a great figure." One moment of such bliss will make you feel it was all worth it. Now, if you are a grandma, don't moan, "I'm too old." Look at Marlene Dietrich and hold your peace. The mother of one of our models recently went from a size sixteen to a ten, with a program of exercise and diet—and went back to work. She is a travel guide and she's

43

in her seventies. Another woman I know who is seventy-nine is in such good shape that she goes on archaeological digs. It's never too late.

Don't be impatient. One week of daily exercising means little, but a month will produce remarkable improvement and six months will turn out a whole new shape.

If you have any special health problems, be sure to speak to your doctor before setting out on an exercise plan. If you check out, read on.

Choose a good spot in your house for your exercising, one with enough space so you won't be bumping into things, and preferably with a cushioning carpet on the floor.

Be sure you are dressed comfortably. Don't wear anything that is tight or binds anywhere at all. Wear something you don't care about, like a pair of comfortable shorts and a stretchy top, or leotards (the best of all), or perhaps your underwear, or nothing at all.

Try working to music. Stack up a pile of rhythmic records on the record player and swing along to the music. Waltzes are best, fast or slow. Adapt the speed to the exercises you are doing. If exercising bores you, do it while the TV or radio is on—you can exercise while part of your mind concentrates on something else.

There are two kinds of exercise, general and specific. The general exercises are good for the entire body, tone up the muscles, and stimulate the circulation. Usually they are the most fun to do. The specific exercises are designed to deal with certain figure problems. With these, you concentrate on specific areas, building up muscles little by little, trimming down flab little by little. With any exercising, start off slowly and work up more speed and the number of exercises gradually. Never allow yourself to become overtired. If a routine seems too strenuous, take time out to relax before starting the next one.

If some exercises bore you, don't do them unless they're essential to your special figure problems. If you like some better than others, stick mostly with these. I'll give you enough so there'll be room for choice. Just keep in mind that the only way you'll have a firm, beautiful body is to stick with it! You'll have a model figure if you're not a quitter. I promise you that.

Now, what are you aiming at? As a general rule, the perfect figure calls for bust and hips to be the same measurement, with the waist ten inches smaller. If bust and hips are 34, then the waist should be 24. Note: your buttocks are an additional measurement. Bring the tape down about three inches below the hipline, around the largest part of the "fanny." This measurement should be approximately two or three inches larger than the hips. Of course, body shapes vary. Some women with a large pelvic structure will find it impossible to keep to the "perfect" formula. Their hips always will be an inch or so larger because you can't whittle down bone. The girl with a large rib cage will find that her waistline may be an inch or so bigger than the so-called ideal. You must work with what you've got.

General Exercises

1

2

1. Running is one of the best all-round body conditioners. If you feel silly running around the block, run around your house, or just run in place for a few minutes.

2. Jumping is another excellent general exercise. Invest in a jump rope, and jump until you can't continue. Start off slowly, and work up to as much as you can take.

45

3. Touch your toes. Raise arms overhead, then bend down, knees straight, and touch your toes with your fingers. Work up from ten bends to about fifty, and gradually try to place your whole palm on the floor in front of your feet.

4. Stretch out. Stand on your tiptoes, legs a bit apart, arms overhead. First stretch one arm up as high as possible, then the other.

46

5. Lie on the floor flat on your back. Legs together, try to lift them straight up in the air. Hold for a few seconds, then lower them slowly. If you can't manage that at first, do it with one leg at a time.

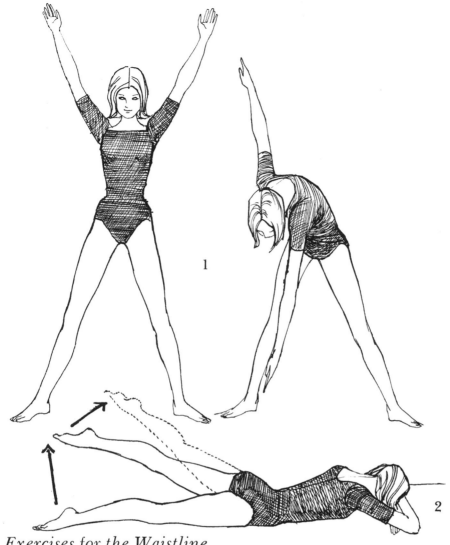

Exercises for the Waistline

1. Stand straight with feet apart and tummy pulled in. Extend your arms overhead and, while keeping arms raised, bend forward and swing left arm until your hand touches your right toe. Return to starting position and repeat with left arm.

2. Lie on floor, face down, with forehead resting on bent arms. Keep your legs out straight. Raise left leg up from the hips, keeping your knee straight, and swing it out to the left as far as possible. Bring back to center position and slowly lower to floor. Repeat exercise with right leg. You should feel the pull on the abdomen and waist.

47

3

4

48

5

3. Take a sitting position, spread-eagle your feet as far apart as possible. Clasp your hands behind your neck, keeping arms and back straight. Now bend and try to touch right elbow to left knee; alternate with left elbow to right knee.

4. Sit erect on stool or bench, with feet firmly on ground, arms stretched out at sides. Twist body from waist up alternately left, right, left, right. Be sure to keep arms at shoulder level throughout this exercise.

5. Sit on the floor, legs in front, back erect, and arms outstretched to the sides at shoulder height. Spread feet apart to form a large V, keeping toes pointed. Bend forward, reaching right hand to left foot, touching your toe. Then touch left hand to right toe. Don't bend arms or legs.

NOTE: In executing all exercises the number of times to do them is left to your own judgment. A good rule to go by is to do each one five times at first, and work up to longer sessions.

49

Exercises for Hips

1. Sit on floor with feet spread apart, legs straight. Lean back on your hands for support. Now, pointing your toes toward the floor, swing your left leg over your right leg, trying to touch the floor on the right side. Reverse and try to carry right leg over left. Do this with a rolling motion so that your hips are moving as you do the exercise. Return to original position after each swing.

2. In this exercise you "walk" on your hips. In a sitting position, stretch legs straight out in front. Now, raise right knee, keeping your right foot on the floor. Then lower right leg, raising left knee and

50

"walking" forward on your hips, shifting weight from one side to the other. Lower left leg and raise right knee. Keep going forward as far as you can, then reverse exercise "walking" backward.

3. In a sitting position, legs stretched out in front, hands in back for support, lift your hips off the floor. Twist to the left, pounding the floor with left hip as hard as you can. Now do the same with the right hip, twisting to the right. As you learn to do this exercise you will pick up speed—the more the better. Here we go, turn left, pound, turn right, pound, back to left, etc.

51

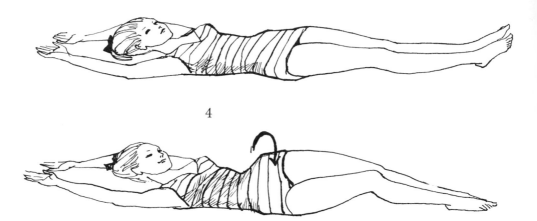

4

4. Down on the floor on your back, stretch arms overhead keeping back and shoulders firm on the floor. Arch your knees slightly and twist your torso as far to the right as you can, being sure to keep back and shoulders still; now twist to the left as far as possible. Alternate right, left, right, left.

5

5. Lie on your side, with one arm tucked under your head, the other keeping your balance. Bring both knees up to your chest. Stretch one leg out parallel to the floor as far as you can, then return it to chest position. Now stretch other leg, return to chest position. Try to do this as rapidly as possible, keeping your hips still as you do the exercise.

6. Lie on back with hands under buttocks. Raise your hips as high off the floor as you can. Bring knees up to chest, then rotate them as though you were riding a bicycle.

7. Sit on floor, back erect. Extend your legs out, also your arms, straight in front of you. Lift legs about three inches from floor and rock back and forth like a rocking chair. Work up to twenty-five times.

53

Exercises for Abdomen

1. Lie flat on floor, arms at sides, with left leg straight and right knee flexed slightly. Slowly raise your head and shoulders, keeping the lower back tight to the floor. Hold this position—this is where the real work begins. Now, try to lift your left leg and thigh as high as possible, being sure to keep your knee straight. Alternate with right leg and thigh. This is a real toughie, so don't be too strenuous about it.

2. Lie flat on floor, feet wide apart. Keep arms outstretched and on a level with your shoulders. Raise head and chest as high as you can, trying

3

4

to keep tummy flat. In this position, swing your left hand toward right knee, then right hand toward left knee. Feel the pull in the stomach muscles?

3. Lie on the floor on your back. Raise your arms overhead, relax knees ever so slightly, keeping soles of feet on the floor. Now, try to raise your hips off the floor, while you pull in your abdomen. Repeat, but go easy on this exercise until you are used to it.

4. Sit on a low stool or bench. Extend your legs in front, placing your feet flat on the floor, tucked under the bed or a heavy chair so they cannot move. With arms folded, bend slowly backward as far as possible. If you can touch the floor with the top of your head, you have mastered the exercise, and this will take *some* doing. Start slowly, once or twice to begin with, finally increasing to ten times.

55

5

6

5. Lie flat on your back. Lift shoulders and legs off the floor simultaneously, and with arms stretched out in front, try to touch your toes. Hold for one or two seconds and return to original position. Repeat.

6. In sitting position on floor, extend arms overhead, keeping them straight, legs straight out in front. Raise your legs up and down alternately, without allowing them to come into contact with the floor throughout the entire exercise.

56

1

Exercises for Diaphragm

The skin in the area of the diaphragm is too delicate to be pounded or bumped away, so to be rid of this excess poundage we must go at it gently. In many cases posture is the culprit, and if your posture is improved the diaphragm line will be slimmed down. When you slump, that area goes into a slump too. The very act of just straightening up will make you look trimmer.

One other thing that helps to flatten you is a good foundation garment. A foundation, fitted properly, will slim you down considerably, *while you have it on.* But I have a few gentle exercises for you—the same ones I give to our models when they first come to our agency. With proper posture and correct weight, our models are not too troubled with this thick diaphragm problem.

1. Lie flat on your back. Raise both legs so that they are at right angles to your body. Relax your knees but do not actually bend them. Now, take hold of your legs at the back, right above the knee joints. With a rocking motion, rock back and forth, forward and backward, until you reach enough momentum to swing you to a half-sitting position with both back and legs off the floor. Hold for a few counts, and rock again. Hold and rock. As you are able to do this exercise more proficiently, you will need fewer rocks to achieve the half-sitting position.

57

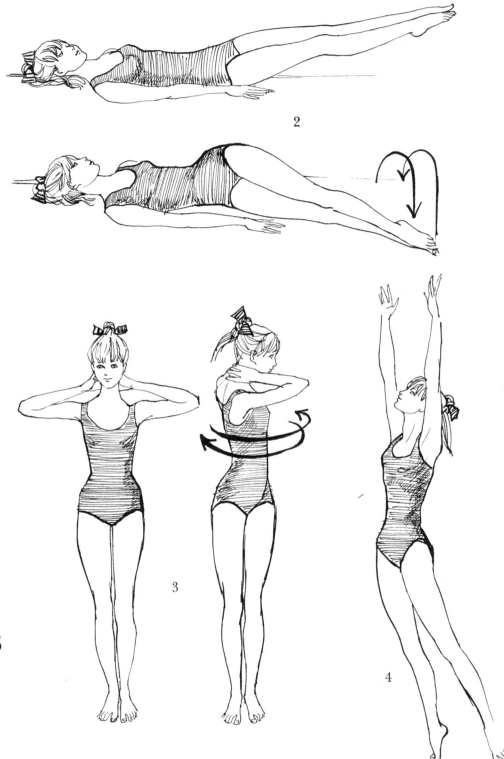

2

3

4

2. Lie on your back with feet slightly off the floor. Swing legs from right to left, and back again, *touching* the floor with each swing. Be sure to keep your back and shoulders flat on the floor.

3. Stand straight with feet apart, clasp your hands at the back of your neck, with elbows level with shoulders. Keeping the lower part of your body still, twist torso to the right as far as possible, bring back to starting position and twist to the left.

4. This one is easy—just stretch, stretch, S-T-R-E-T-C-H. When you get out of bed in the morning, take time to stretch, arms up, as high as you can reach, then relax, then stretch again. Pull your waist up out of your hips.

Exercises for Arms

For overplump or sagging arm muscles, turn to Chapter 9.

Exercises for Legs

See next chapter.

Now that you've read all the exercises, it's time to try them. Don't collapse in discouragement—you are not expected to do all of them. Select the exercises that apply to your particular problems and forget the others, except the general tone-up group. Get out your checklist of areas that need improvement, and, as the weeks go by, mark in the changes in your measurements. I've given you plenty of choice in exercises, so you can vary your routine as you wish. Now's the time to get going. Put on your leotards, pick your spot, and get started! You're on the way to a brand-new figure.

8
Leg Work – How the Models Do It

To be a model, you must have good legs. Many a girl, though otherwise quite beautiful, has been rejected by our agency because her legs were not great. Some girls are used only for head shots because of this. But all of our girls, who have pretty legs now, didn't always have them. Sometimes, they had to work on them to bring them up to snuff. I'm going to tell you how they did it with exercise.

But first, the cosmetic approach. Even perfect legs require attention. It's strange that women will spend hours in front of a mirror working on their makeup and hairdos, yet their legs and feet somehow get left out of their beauty programs. A beauty is beautiful all over. If you maintain a year-round vigilance, you'll be delighted when summer comes and your legs and feet are on display. Here's what our models must do for their legs.

1. Legs must be free of hair. There are different ways of accomplishing this. There is the shaving method which, to me, is the least practical method as it has to be done frequently, often leaves nicks and scratches, and the hair grows in again in a dark, prickly stubble. If you do shave, do it on soapy wet legs against the grain of the hair, and cream your skin afterward. The second method of hair removal is with wax, which is melted, applied while warm to the legs, and allowed to harden. Then the wax is pulled off like adhesive tape and the hair, with its roots, is pulled off with it. Ouch! My objections to this method are that it hurts, the hair has to be a certain length before the treatment is effective, and the in-between period is pretty unattractive. The effect does last a few weeks, however, and there won't be a stubble.

My favorite method, the third, is the depilatory. This is a cream that is applied to the legs, then rinsed off—do it before you get into the tub.

61

The hair comes off with it. Even though most of these creams have an unattractive scent, I find them preferable to shaving or waxing. You'll need to use one about once every two weeks. One word of caution: make a patch test to see if you are allergic to any new depilatory before you use it.

2. While in the bath, give your legs a gentle going over with a wet pumice stone to remove dead skin.

3. Treat them to a daily rubdown with body lotion after your bath. This keeps the skin smooth and moist.

Leg Contouring

Is it possible to improve the contours of your legs? Yes, it is. Heavy legs can be streamlined and skinny calves can be filled out. Ankles can be trimmed, flabby thighs can be firmed up. Obviously, some of us—despite all our efforts—will have to go through life with less than perfect legs because many problems—like heavy bones or bowed legs—cannot be corrected. But all problem legs can be improved *with exercise,* regular exercise. You can train and maintain your leg muscles, and I am going to give you the exercises used by my models to help you do just that.

General Exercises

1. Stand barefoot on the floor with feet separated, say fifteen inches. Rise on the balls of your feet, turn your body from the waist up, to the right. Bend knees and slowly lower yourself to the floor. Straighten up to original position, and repeat, turning to the left. This exercise takes a bit of doing, especially if your balance is not the greatest.

2. Sit on a chair. Kick as high as you can, first with your left leg, keeping toes pointed out straight ahead. Pull foot toward you as you lower leg. Repeat with right leg. You should feel a pull in the calf muscles.

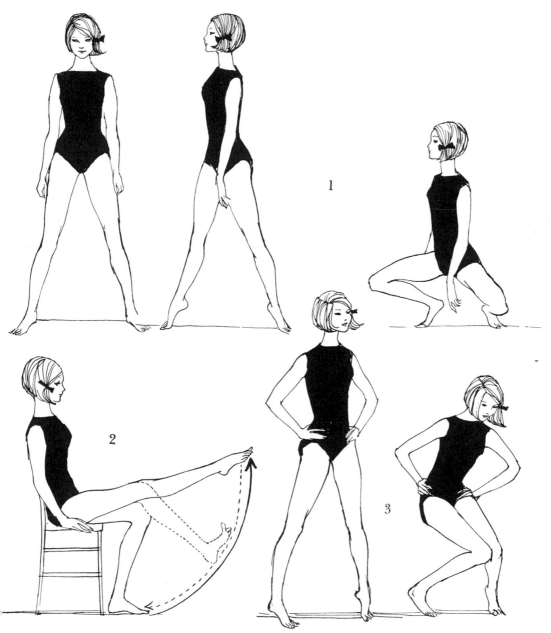

1

2

3

3. This is another balance exercise, for strengthening muscles. Stand pigeon-toed, feet slightly apart, hands on hips. Rise to the balls of your feet, bend your knees, sinking slowly until the knees touch. This exercise may seem difficult at first, but keep at it.

63

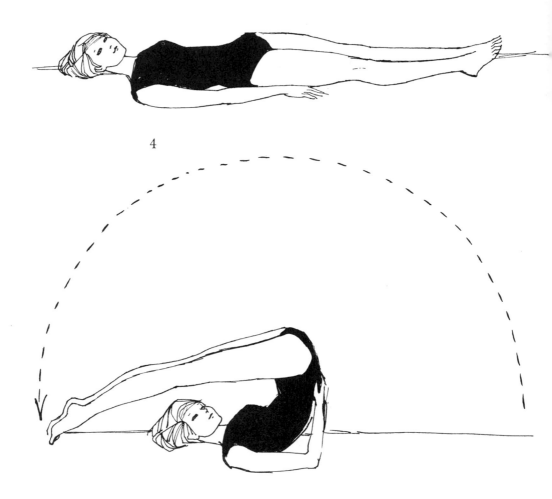

4. Lie on back, with arms at sides; swing your legs up over your head, trying to touch the floor behind your head. Use your hands to support your hips, if necessary.

5. Lie on your side, with lower arm stretched up over your head. Place free arm on the floor in front of your chest. Now, slowly pull your knees up to your chest and snap them out quickly. Roll over on the other side and repeat action. Do this ten times on each side.

6. Stand straight, feet parallel, about three inches apart. Bend body forward, raising left leg backward and up. Stretch your arms to the side, and hold this position; then repeat exercise with right leg.

5

6

65

To Mold and Strengthen Calves

1. Stand with feet turned out, keeping body erect. Squat on haunches. Hold arms out to sides like a Siamese dancer and jump forward four times. Hold. Repeat until you can go across room without stopping.

2. Place your toes and the balls of your feet on a book about one-inch thick, keeping your heels on the floor. As you raise heels off the floor, breathe in at the count of one, raising your hands to shoulder level. Go up and up, to the count of five. Then, descend slowly, lowering arms to sides. As you become more adept at this exercise, increase the thickness of the book one-half inch at a time until it reaches three inches.

3. Stand with your feet together, hands on hips. Jump, spreading your feet about eighteen inches apart; then jump back to original position. Do this twenty-five times or more, morning and night.

4. Place hands on back of a chair. Slowly sink toward the floor, keeping your weight on the balls of your feet, toes turned in, heels in the air, until your bent knees are well forward of your toes and arms are bent. Then straighten arms and legs without letting heels touch the floor. Work up to ten times morning and night.

67

5. Stand straight. Clasp your hands behind your head. Slowly sink down until your knees are bent and your heels are raised almost an inch from the floor. Return slowly to erect position. Repeat. Work up to ten times.

7

6. With right hand holding on to chair, and left arm extended out from shoulder, extend left leg back, toes on floor, and bounce, not jump, on your toes four times. Then sink down on right leg to crouch position. Left arm should sink forward and head hang forward on chest. Then straighten up, pushing with right leg, until body is returned to position. Alternate four times each leg.

7. Assume same position as number six. Bounce six times. On seventh count, kick left leg forward keeping body erect. Bring back for the eighth count. Repeat and on the seventh count kick with knee bent and chest bent toward each other. Return on eighth count. Alternate four complete exercises on each leg.

8

8. Stand facing back of chair, holding on with both hands. Pretend you are a scissor. Put one leg, scissor fashion, in back of the other. Now jump, keeping weight on toes, reversing legs to this count: one group of four jumps, four groups of two jumps, six groups of one jump.

9. Sit on the floor, legs separated about six inches. Bend your knees and draw back your heels up close to the hips, lean back on your hands. Slap knees and calves together so that you can feel them tingle. This should be done one hundred times a day—fifty in the morning and another fifty at night.

9

10

10. Squat, with your arms between your knees, hands on floor, palms down. Straighten up your legs, pushing forward, so that the weight of the body is on the hands. Your knees and elbows should be straight. Drop to original position and repeat slowly fifteen times.

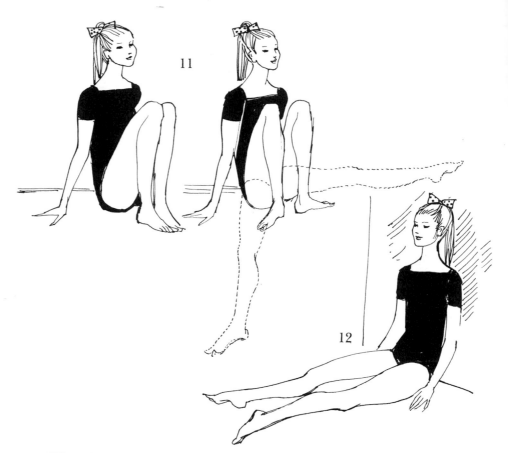

These last two exercises can help bow legs, not by changing the bone structure, which is impossible, but by developing the inner calves to produce an optical illusion. If you fill out your thin legs, the gap is less noticeable.

11. Sit on the floor, resting weight on your hands behind your hips. Keep feet on the floor, bend your knees and draw your legs up close to the buttocks. Now turn knees and toes out slowly, slide legs forward while turning your calves toward each other. Push legs out as far as you can, stretching them at the same time. Hold tight and count to twenty.

12. Sit on the floor with your back against a heavy chair or the wall. Extend your legs straight out in front of you, heels together. Roll each leg outward and try to make your calves meet. Stretch your toes. Hold this position, slowly counting to ten. Do you feel that stretch in the calf muscles? Now relax and repeat.

To Slim Ankles

1. Lie on your back with one foot high in the air, keeping your knee straight. Now slowly outline ten large circles with your big toe, going first to the right, then to the left. Alternate your feet. Be sure that the action is with the foot only; do not move your leg.

2. Stand with your palms against the wall. Rise up on your toes and drop down to your heels. Do this twenty-five times just as fast as you can—up and down, up and down.

3. Stand with feet flat on the floor. Raise your heels so that you are way up on your toes. Slap heels back to floor with a real snap.

4. Here is a massaging exercise to slim your ankles. Lie on the floor. Grasp one ankle firmly with both hands, and with a twisting motion, twist from front to back of ankle. Continue this squeezing and wringing motion up through the calf of the leg. Rest and repeat with other leg. DO these exercises, don't just read about them!

5. Sit on a chair and cross your left leg over your right knee. Point your toes up, heel down, then curl toes under and make five circles to the right and then five circles to the left. Cross your right leg over your left knee and repeat with right foot.

6. Sit on the floor with legs extended in front of you, leaning back on your hands. Bend your toes toward you as far as possible, and then away from you—toward you and back, toward you and back, five times.

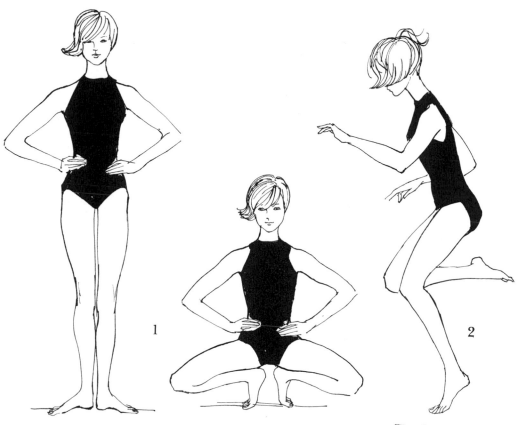

1

2

7. Lie on your back. Curl your toes under and clench firmly. As you grip, push your foot forward at the ankle and push down with your heels. Repeat five times, relax, and repeat five more times.

To Slim Down Thighs

1. Standing erect, hands on hips, heels together and toes pointed out, rise on your toes and slowly lower your body to a squatting position. Return *slowly* to starting position. If you wish, use a chair to balance yourself at first, until you are able to squat without the aid of a prop.

2. Hop on right foot six times, then change and hop on left foot. This can be done with a jumping rope if you like, hopping twice or more on one foot, then the other.

3

4

5

76

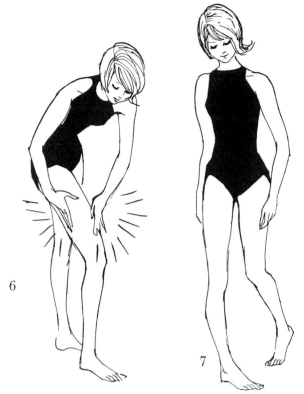

6

7

3. Stand straight, arms loosely at sides. Bend knees, keeping buttocks tucked under, tummy in, back straight. Do this bend as low as you can. Return to starting position and repeat.

4. Stand erect, feet slightly apart. Count four slowly. Step out to the left on left foot and lunge, bending knee. Keep body facing front. Hold for a count of four, then slowly draw up to count of four, keeping weight on right foot. Remain for count of four, then lunge to right.

5. Hold back of chair with left hand. Bend knee and balance on ball of left foot. Extend right leg straight back of left, keeping some weight on ball of right foot. Bounce up and down four times, then kick forward and up with right leg. Alternate legs.

6. This time you are going to give your thighs a "beating" by slapping them with your open palms. In standing position, bend forward and slap thighs with your palms, using both hands and concentrating on one thigh at a time. Slap, slap, slap, both sides, then one side with both hands. Be brisk with your slaps—no wishy-washy little taps here. Keep doing this until your hands are tired. This will bring up the circulation!

7. Walk around the room ten times, toes pointed way in.

77

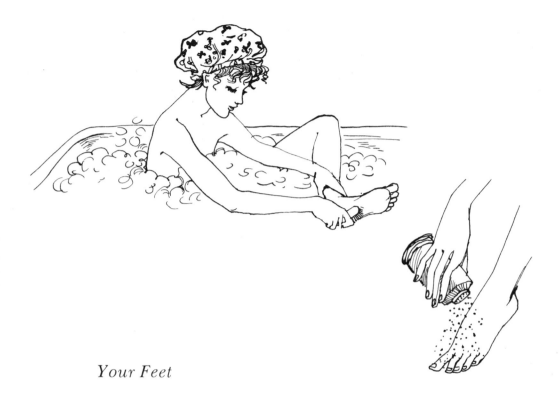

Your Feet

For some reason, probably because women think their feet are rarely on display, these extremities usually are sadly neglected by otherwise well-groomed girls. But your feet should not only look as pretty as you can make them, they should feel good, too. Nothing can put a strain on your face—or on your back—like a pair of hurting feet. Your walk is a vital part of your appearance, and if your feet ache, you won't be very graceful.

Follow these rules and your feet will hold you up happily.

1. Keep them clean. During your daily bath, scrub your feet with a brush, especially the soles. Go over the heels and soles and any other rough parts with a wet pumice stone in a round-and-round motion; then go around the edges and under the toenails with an orange stick to help prevent ingrown toenails. Dry your feet thoroughly, particularly between the toes—athlete's foot loves dampness. Push back your cuticles with a towel. Now smooth on body lotion, and when it's dry, dust with back powder, being sure to get some between each toe.

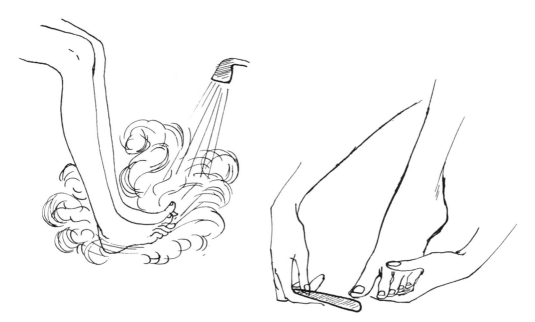

2. If your feet perspire excessively, wash them a second time each day and change your stockings. Dust your feet and your shoes with antiseptic powder. Or try a spray-on deodorant before applying the powder. Try nylons with cotton feet.

3. Always buy shoes that fit you perfectly. More damage to feet is done by bad shoes than anything else. Be sure they are large enough, but not too large. Avoid very pointed toes that pinch, or flat toes that press down. If you start to get a rubbed spot on your foot, don't wear those shoes again for at least a week. Then try them again. Vary your heel heights so that your feet don't become too accustomed to only one. Never go without stockings or peds or socks to absorb moisture. As for corns and calluses and the like, I suggest only pads to remove pressure. Beyond that, I don't think you should fool around yourself—go to a reputable podiatrist and do as he suggests.

4. Give yourself a pedicure as often as your toenails need cutting or your polish chips. Here's how to do it: first remove all old polish with oily polish remover. Then cut your toenails straight across with a toenail scissors. Smooth nails with an emery board. Never cut nails down at the sides or you'll be inviting ingrown toenails. Push back cuticles after applying cuticle cream.

79

Now soak feet in warm water for about three minutes. Dry thoroughly and give them a vigorous massage with body lotion.

To apply polish, keep your toes separated with cotton. Apply polish first across the base of the nail with one stroke and then work from the bottom up. You'll find that two coats look better than one. Finally, apply a sealer coat and allow to dry thoroughly before removing the cotton.

5. Relieve tired feet by pampering them. You'll find some of the following exercises will help them relax. But if your feet are hot and weary, sit on the edge of the bathtub and run first hot water, then cold over them. Alternate the water this way for a few minutes. Or soak them in warm water to which you've added a couple of tablespoons of bicarbonate of soda, baking soda, or Epsom salts. When you're finished and have dried your feet, apply body lotion generously and give your feet a good massage. Then lie down with your feet higher than your hips (preferably higher than your head if you can manage that) for at least ten minutes.

Exercises for the Feet

If your feet are to give you the best possible service, you must exercise them. I heard someone say that most people give their feet less care than they give the tires of their car—and yet you chalk up more miles in a lifetime than your car does. Besides, you can't replace your feet.

Because our models must, on occasion, stand up for twelve or more hours a day, they can't afford to have complaining feet. Here are some of the exercises we recommend to them to strengthen the foot muscles and to give the feet a chance to "breathe":

1. Walk barefoot around the room. Then stand on your tiptoes, stretching your arms high at the same time. Drop down, walk around some more, and repeat the stretching.

2. Stand straight with feet parallel. Roll your feet out to the sides, putting weight on the outer edges. Curl down the toes, trying to keep them touching the floor. Walk in this position for ten minutes a day—or more if you can. You'll find this will help to strengthen your arches.

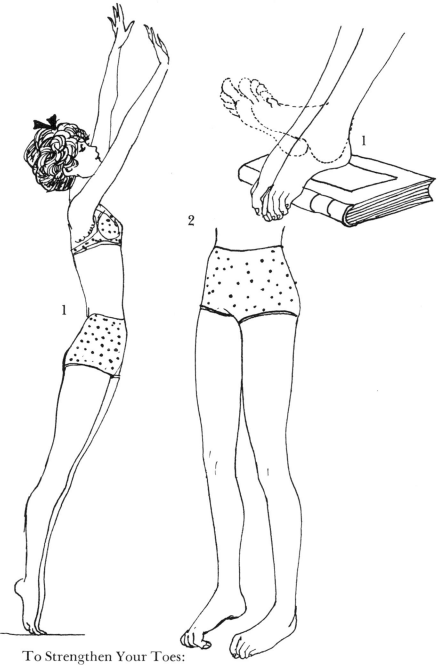

To Strengthen Your Toes:

1. Sit erect with feet on a book—keep them parallel, about five inches apart. Extend the toes over the front edge, bending them down as far as possible. Then raise them as high as you can. Now try to raise your feet high, keeping your heels on the book, then lower to original position. Repeat until the muscles tire.

2. Stand with feet slightly apart. First rise onto your toes, with heels off the floor. Hold this position for a minute, then rock back on heels and raise toes off the floor. Repeat several times.

3. Strew some marbles or nuts on the floor and try to pick them up with your toes. A pencil will do, too.

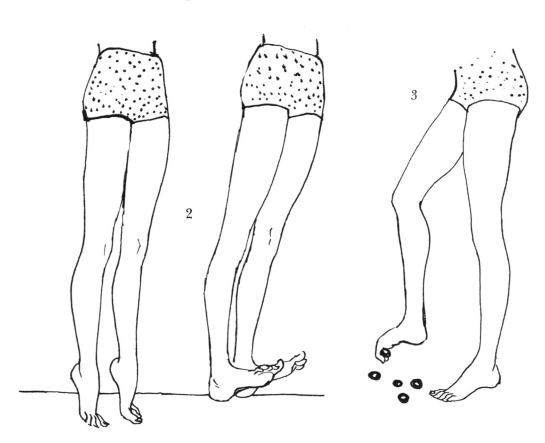

9

My Recipe for Good-Looking Arms

I hope you haven't reached the point where your upper arms have (suddenly, you say?) become loose and flabby—because it's a lot easier to prevent this problem than it is to cure it. But don't lose heart—it's quite possible to rectify the situation. Both preventing and rectifying require exercise. These same exercises will work to slim down

heavy arms (by getting rid of the fat tissue) as well as round out skinny arms (by building up muscle).

If your arms haven't become flabby, now is the time to make sure you won't have that unattractive muscle sag, which is the plague of so many women over that "certain age." My exercises will not be an absolute guarantee against flabby arms, but they will help to tone and firm the underarm muscles so that there will be much less chance for it to happen. They will keep your arms toned and firmed. Have you ever noticed how nicely rounded the arms of a waitress are? This is because carrying large and heavy trays all day long strengthens and builds up the arm muscles. I'm going to give you my special set of exercises so that you can put off the day when you'll feel more comfortable wearing long sleeves.

First, be sure you've done right by the skin on your arms. This area, too, needs beauty care. Rub body lotion on your arms as well as the rest of you, every day, after your bath. Have you looked at your elbows lately? If they are rough and dark, I suggest using cuticle remover. Soak a piece of cotton in remover and apply to your elbows, letting it soak into the skin for several minutes. Then rub off the dead skin. Soak your elbows in oil once a week to keep them soft.

If you are troubled by a lot of hair on your arms, something can be done about that, too. Bleach it to make it less noticeable—using an oil bleach available at the drugstore. Or if it's very heavy, you may prefer a depilatory. A more extreme solution is electrolysis—removal of the hairs by an expert using an electric needle. A liquid foundation matched to your skin tone can cover brown spots that sometimes occur.

Now for the exercises. Do all of these standing up.

1. Stand straight, with arms lifted above your head and stretched up high. Take a deep breath, then bring arms down to shoulder level as you bend forward at the waist. Pull your arms back as far as possible. Hold for a few seconds, then raise body slowly, keeping arms back. Exhale slowly as you straighten up.

2. Standing, place fingertips lightly on your shoulders. Now rotate your elbows, making large circles first to the back, then to the front—slowly.

3. Stretch arms overhead. Keeping left arm up and your body as straight as you can, slowly turn head to the right, at the same time lowering right arm and stretching it as far back as possible. Hold for a count of five. Return to original position slowly. Repeat with left arm.

85

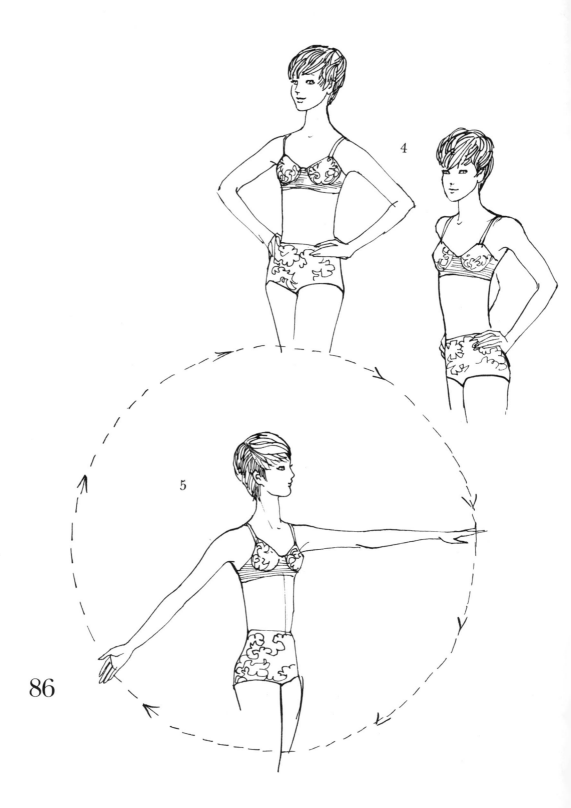

4

5

86

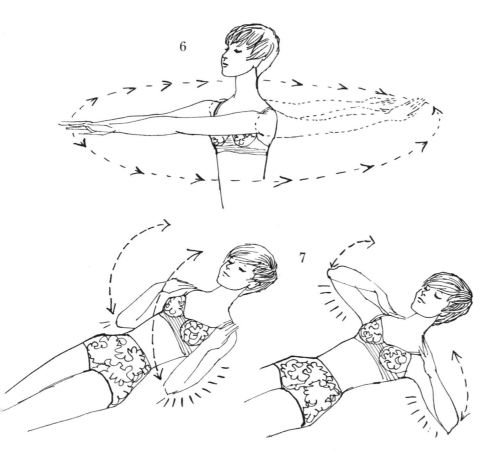

4. Stand with hands on hips. Push elbows as far back as they will go. Bring them forward and repeat.

5. Stretch arms forward at shoulder height. Raise right arm and make a large circle, first in one direction, then in the other, returning to forward position. Now do the same with left arm. Alternate until you are tired.

6. Stretch arms forward at shoulder height. Swing them apart and back, trying to touch fingertips as they meet behind your back.

Now lie down.

7. Flat on your back, place fingertips lightly on shoulders, elbows by your side. Raise elbows high and slap your arms down hard. Repeat several times. Then, with fingertips still on shoulders, move elbows out so that the undersides of the arms touch the floor. Slap them on the floor.

87

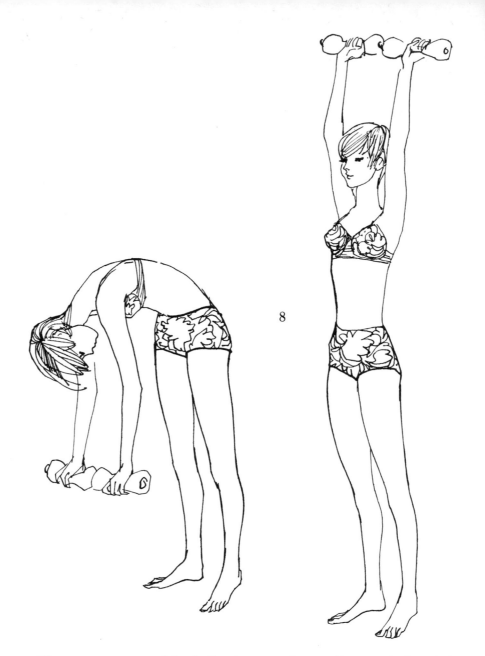

8

Have you ever used barbells—I mean the small ones designed for women? They can be most helpful for firming up your arms. Try these two exercises:

8. Stand with feet about a foot apart. Grasp bells in your hands, bend forward, keeping legs straight, arms hanging down. Now raise up, swing arms forward and up overhead. Swing back to original position.

9. Lie flat on the bed, with your head slightly extended over the edge. Hold the barbells and start with arms straight down at your sides. Now raise your arms over your head, as far back as possible. You can feel the pull in the underarm muscles. Hold for a few seconds, then slowly return arms back to original position.

These barbell exercises will tire you at first but just do them a few times in the beginning and gradually work up to more—that's a good idea for any exercise, so that your muscles can slowly become used to their new way of life without too much protest.

10
Put Up a Good Front

Now everyone knows that most fashion models tend to be a bit lacking when it comes to bosoms. That's because they must be really slim in order to photograph well. But models accept this fact of their lives, and are always equipped with a variety of falsies. And they know how to make the most of what they've got. I'm going to tell you how they do it.

If you are not as full-breasted as you'd like to be, you have to realize that there isn't much you can do to increase your measurements except to gain weight. Breasts contain no muscles—they are made up of glands and fat. They are, however, supported by a network of muscles and ligaments, and it is these muscles that can be strengthened so that your breasts will look their best. Sagging breasts can be prevented by proper care throughout your life, and they can be raised by proper exercising and posture. Oversized breasts can be reduced only by losing weight. Of course, both small and large breasts can be improved by plastic surgery—but that's another story and we'll get to that later.

Before we get to the work, let's consider a few other things. Be sure you are wearing the correct brassiere, with enough support. This is best decided by an experienced corsetiere. Even small breasts can sag eventually if they are not properly supported. Go to a good corsetiere if you have trouble finding bras that support, fit well, and are comfortable. A good bra, besides giving support, can also give your bosom a pretty shape. Many girls today do not wear bras at all—but this is not a good idea unless you have a *very* boyish bosom that *really* needs no support.

Check your weight. If you are your proper weight there's nothing more you can do to change the size of your breasts. If your weight changes, be sure to check your bra size—too tight bras can break down tissues and cause eventual sagging; too loose don't give enough support. Don't lose weight too fast, or your skin (and not just on your breasts) will not keep pace, resulting in flabbiness.

Posture has a great deal to do with the appearance of your bosom. Round your shoulders and notice what happens. A general sag. Now throw your shoulders back, pull in your tummy, and you look completely different.

The importance of correct breathing can't be overestimated. Breathing the right way helps to develop the chest and shoulder muscles, which in turn raise the breasts for a prettier bust line. Deep breathing is not something to do only before breakfast and before you go to bed. You should make a habit of taking deep breaths, expanding your lungs, several times a day.

91

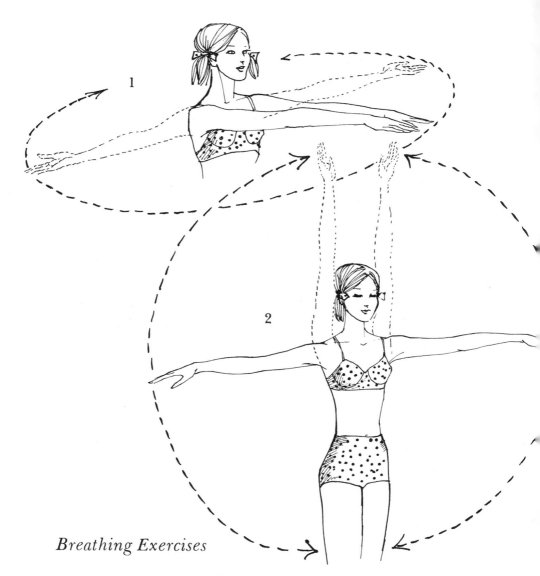

Breathing Exercises

1. Stand straight in front of an open window (weather and neighbors permitting), head and shoulders back, chin up. Extend arms forward, shoulder height, with palms down. Slowly start to inhale as you move your arms back. When they are in a line with your shoulders, turn palms upward, hold a second, then continue as far back as you can reach. Hold a few seconds, then exhale as you return to your original position.

2. Again in front of the window, hands at sides, inhale and raise arms slowly to the sides until they reach over your head. Stop for a

second at shoulder level and hold your breath. Then continue on up. Hold breath a few seconds, then lower arms, exhaling.

3. Stand with knees flexed. Inhale deeply, raise chest, and hold for several seconds. Exhale and repeat.

4. Lie on the floor with arms stretched above head. Take a deep breath, hold, and stretch. Exhale.

Exercises for the Bust Line

Start slowly because you may be using muscles that have been inactive for years. These will tone and firm the supporting muscles of the chest and shoulders.

1. Stand straight, hands on hips with thumbs toward the front. Swing elbows back, trying to make them touch. Slack slightly, then snap backward several times before returning to normal position.

2. Stand, arms raised to the sides, level with shoulders, fingertips on shoulders. Move elbows forward so that they meet in front of chest. Bring elbows upward and then backward as far as possible so that you feel a pull in the chest muscles. Now bring elbows downward and forward to touch again in front. In other words, make a circle with your elbows. Repeat several times.

3

4

5

94

6

3. Stand with arms at sides, feet about twelve inches apart. Keep left arm at side, move right arm backward and upward to shoulder level—do not twist the body. Hold position for several seconds, then slowly continue upward movement keeping arm straight and as close to head as you can until it is directly overhead. Hold, then bring arm slowly forward and downward in front of face, crossing over so that your right hand touches left wrist. Return to the original position, and repeat using left arm.

4. Standing straight, stretch arms overhead with palms facing and about twelve inches apart. Push your arms as far back as you can. Do this several times: then widen space to about four inches and push back. Keep widening space, then pushing back until you have about two feet between palms. Drop arms to original position.

5. The breaststroke can be done *out* of water as well as in a pool. Stand straight, arms at sides. Extend arms forward and raise to shoulder level, palms out. Move your arms to the side in an arc. Then drop elbows and bring palms of hands together in front of chest, then shoot them forward to first position. Turn palms out and repeat.

6. Tired? Let's sit down for a while. In sitting position, place right fist in left palm. With left arm push right arm to right side, resisting with right arm. Done correctly you will notice an uplifting of the breast. Now, with right arm push left arm to left side. Repeat several times.

7. At shoulder height, place right hand on left arm a few inches below the elbow. Left hand on right arm. Press hands outward with a firm grip toward the elbows.

8. Same position, with legs crossed. Cross your arms and rest them on your knees. Now, vigorously swing your arms into a wide V over your head. Bring back to starting position and repeat.

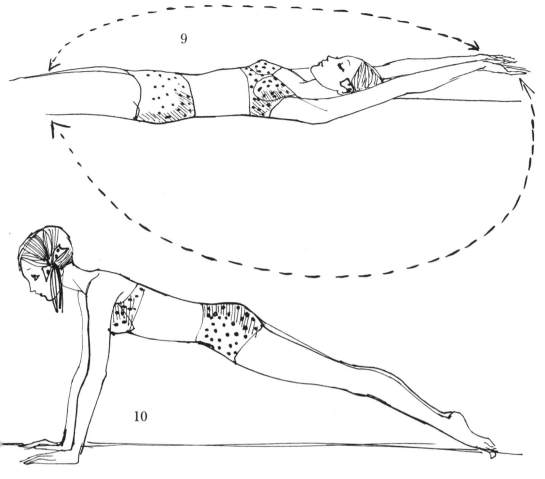

9. Lie on the floor with arms resting at sides. Lift your arms slowly upward and on over your head, keeping elbows straight until fingertips are a few inches from floor. Swing arms slowly sideways, and describing an arc bring them back to sides in original position.

10. Push-ups will help firm chest muscles. Lie flat on the floor on your tummy, hands on floor just outside the bosom. Push body straight up with hands, keeping knees still, till body rests on hands and toes. Lower and repeat.

In order to have a beautiful bosom, you must not have round shoulders. Try these exercises to develop the beautiful carriage that is required of all models.

97

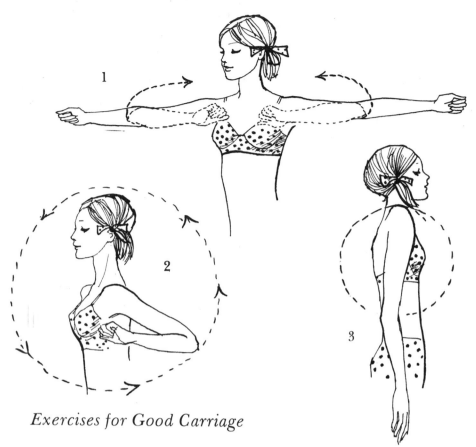

Exercises for Good Carriage

1. Stand with feet together, arms out at sides at shoulder level. Clench fists and bring them forward holding them lightly against chest. Swing elbows back vigorously, then snap forward to first position. Repeat several times.

2. In same arm position, bend elbows, rotate them, making arcs in one direction, then in the other. Keep elbows up but do not lift shoulders.

3. Stand with hands at sides. Rotate right shoulder from back to front describing as large a circle as possible. Then from front to back. Alternate same movement with left shoulder. After doing exercise with each shoulder separately, do it with both shoulders at the same time.

4. Use your barbells. Stand straight, holding weights out to the sides at shoulder level, keeping arms straight. Now move weights backward in large circles. Can't you feel the back shoulder muscles getting a workout?

Be sure that the weight on the barbell is suitable for you. Start with a
light weight and gradually increase, as your muscles become more tuned
to the use of the bells.

5. Raise arms to the sides at shoulder level. Swing them down so
that they cross in front. Snap them back up to shoulder level, making a
big arc in front of you.

99

11
Pose or Posture–
Affect and Effect

Next time you walk past a store window or a full-length mirror, take a glimpse at yourself. Are you walking with your head high, your tummy flat, your bottom tucked under? Are your shoulders thrown back? Or are you slouching along? Bad posture can destroy the whole effect of a beautiful woman, though she may have a sensational figure.

The dictionary defines posture as signifying "state of mind or attitude." When you slouch around, the impression you create is one of an attitude of depression, sadness, lack of confidence. When you stand up straight, you look certain, healthy, and much happier. How often have you tried on a dress you've seen on someone else—perhaps a model—the same size you are, and discovered to your dismay that it didn't look well on you at all? Chances are your posture is the culprit. Models must learn how to carry themselves correctly before they get to the point where they can arrange themselves into those often outlandish positions you see in the fashion magazines. And the models who show clothes on a runway have spent many long hours on their posture.

Poor posture can adversely affect your circulation, breathing, your bone alignment, and even your digestion, because you are forcing your internal organs out of position. You may have backaches or your feet may hurt. When you stand straight, your whole body functions better. You have more energy and your body does not tire so quickly.

How can you tell if you have good posture? Here is my test for it. Stand in front of a full-length mirror stripped naked as Venus Rising From the Sea, and give yourself a good looking over. Do your shoulders droop, do you sag in the middle, pushing out your stomach? Does your head jut out in front, derriere behind? Your posture is in need of immediate repair. Another way to test your stance is to face a wall with chest and toes touching it. Does your nose touch too? If so, you are holding your head too far forward. If your tummy touches, your fanny is thrust out too far and your abdominal muscles are not working properly.

Here's the proper way to stand: pretend there is a loop on the top of your head, in line with your ears. Attached to the loop is a string stretching straight up. This lifts your head back and out of your shoulders. Keeping shoulders back, not stiffly but relaxed, raise your rib cage and pull your tummy in and up into the rib cage. At the same time, tuck your derriere under as far as you can. Don't keep your arms and legs stiff, but slightly flexed, and natural. Your feet should point straight ahead.

101

You'll find that this posture will make you look slimmer and much more graceful. Your waistline will actually be smaller.

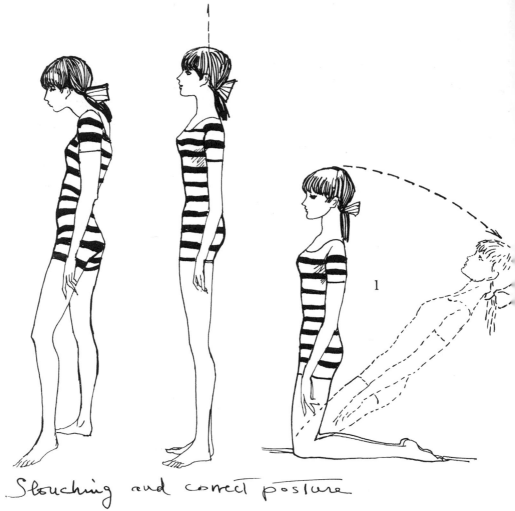

Slouching and correct posture

Try the models' trick: stand with your back against the wall so that your heels, small of the back, shoulder blades, and head touch; there will be just a small hollow at your back. Lift up the rib cage and walk slowly away from the wall. This may seem a strain at first, but that's because you've been giving in to bad habits for so long that you don't feel comfortable or natural when you are standing correctly. But with practice, it will be easier to maintain for longer periods of time as your muscles become accustomed to their new alignment.

102

Now, with all these instructions, you might end up looking stiff and tense. Consciously try to be relaxed about it. It will come naturally after a while.

Here are some general exercises for posture improvement:

1. Kneel on the floor, then sit on your heels. Now rise up to a kneeling position, keeping back straight so that the torso is at right angles to the floor. Slowly bend body as far back as you can, keeping back straight. Return to starting position and repeat.

2. Stand erect with feet apart, arms straight out to the sides at shoulder height. Twist to the left and bend, trying to touch your left toe with your right hand. Straighten up. Now twist to the right, touching right toe with left hand.

3. Stand straight, arms relaxed at your sides. Raise arms slowly to the sides, straight up over your head. Clasp hands and bend slowly to the right, keeping tummy in and chest high. Now to the left. Lower arms.

103

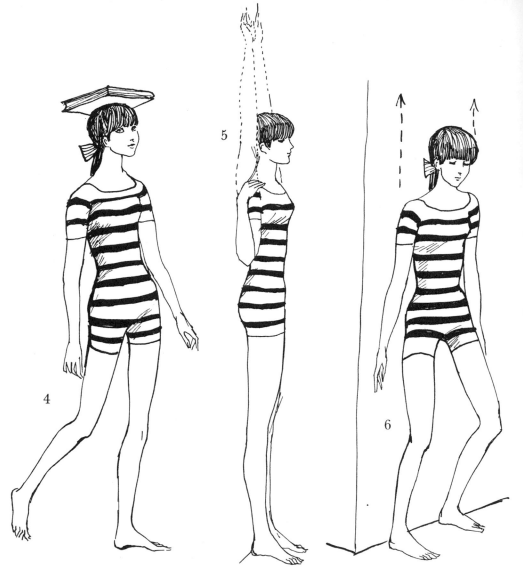

4. Place a book on the top of your head and walk around the room. If your head isn't held straight, your chin up, the book will fall off.

5. Stand with your back to the wall. Place your hands on your shoulders, keeping elbows close to the body. Slowly raise your arms above your head, keeping elbows against the wall. Bring hands back to shoulders.

6. Stand with your back to the wall, feet a few inches apart. Bend knees and rotate thighs outward so that you feel the end of your spine being tucked under. Press the small of your back to the wall, then follow with shoulders, then head, keeping chin in. As you "crawl" up the wall, try to straighten your knees. Hold position for a count of fifteen.

7. Lie on the floor on your back, arms at sides. Bend knees and bring feet up to the buttocks. Now tip pelvis up, pressing the small of the back to the floor. Pull in abdomen. Hold, then relax.

8. Sit on the floor with your legs crossed. Jut your head forward, keeping shoulders back and relaxed. Now bring your chin down and in, and at the same time, draw your head back into an erect position. While in this position, move your head slightly from side to side, keeping chin in a line with shoulders.

9. Sit on the floor, legs straight out in front. Place your hands on the floor behind your hips. With your weight on your hands and heels, legs straight, lift hips as high as you can. Hold, lower your hips, and repeat.

Try to remember that you probably won't work miracles immediately—but after all, it took you years to get that way!

12
Wise Walking and Pretty Sitting

Do you walk gracefully? Do you have a really good idea of how you walk? Most women don't, and yet the manner in which you handle your body in the process of getting from one place to another is very important. One of the first things our models must learn is how to walk correctly—a graceful, free-swinging gait is a real beauty asset. I am not referring to the manner in which mannequins saunter across the platform at a fashion opening. Remember that these shows are just that—shows. The idea is to display the gowns, and to do this a certain amount of showmanship is necessary. It may take an exaggerated glide or gesture or turn to center attention on special detail in the dress, but try these same tricks walking down the street and you'd look nothing less than ridiculous. So, in training our models, I teach them how to walk correctly at all times, even if they're only going down the street to the corner grocery.

A person's walk is most revealing. If you watch someone go down the street, you subconsciously form an opinion of that person because it reflects her personality, her state of mind, and her health. She will look serene, poised, full of tensions, angry, elegant—any number of things.

What impression do you give as you step out for a stroll? Have you noticed any of these (of course, none of them will be *you!*) ?

The scurrier. This is the woman who scurries along with short, mincing steps, neck forward, leading with the chin. She looks smug and self-satisfied, not particularly pleasant to know. To correct this head-separated-from-the-shoulders look, this lady should slow down, take longer steps, draw her head back, and keep her chin parallel to the floor.

The aggressive type. She has her eye on where she is headed and makes straight for the target, looking neither right nor left and stepping

107

aside for no one. Arms swinging, chest thrown out, her attitude fairly screams: "Here I come, get out of my way." Her shoulders should be relaxed, her stride shortened, her arms slowed down.

The shy one. With head down and bent slightly forward, she glances furtively from side to side as though someone were about to jump at her. She should hold her head up, making believe that a string attached at the top is pulling higher, higher, higher. Usually this kind of person holds her arms pressed tightly to her sides—she should let them swing freely from the body.

The swinger. This girl sways from side to side as she walks along, her hips shifting with each step. This is guaranteed to attract attention, all right, but not the kind you want. To diminish the hip movement, try walking along two imaginary lines, or actually draw two lines close together on the floor. With each step, walk so that the knees brush lightly.

The sloucher. This poor soul has a tired, worn manner. Feet and

head are held forward and the torso is relaxed into a big letter *C*. It makes you tired just to watch her. To change this, the sloucher should stand tall and place her weight on the balls of the feet. The tips of the ears should be just above the small hollow in the shoulder bone.

From these few examples, perhaps you recognize some people you know—or even yourself. Get in the habit of checking up on the way you walk. Your body should move rhythmically, with legs swinging forward from your hip joints, not from the knees alone. Remember that your legs should precede you as you walk. This will help to keep your buttocks where they belong—*under* you, not pushed out behind. As you step, place your foot on the ground with the heel touching first, the weight at the outside of the foot. Then the ball of the foot comes down. This is done so quickly it seems to be one action, but actually there are three separate movements.

Your arms should move in the opposite direction to that of your legs. A correct step is approximately the length of your shoe or a trifle longer. Keep your movements easy and relaxed. Check up on your posture—that is vital to an attractive walk.

Ask a friend to watch you and tell you the truth about your gait. Watch yourself as you walk along next to a reflecting store window or use a full-length mirror—all of these will help you find out how you walk. Also try to listen to your footsteps. Do you hear a clickety-clack behind you? Perhaps you need shoes that will stay on your heels. Or do you hear a scuffling, indicating that you are barely lifting your feet off the ground? Do your feet come down on the pavement with a heavy clump, clump, clump?

Remember: point your toes straight ahead, let your knees brush as you walk, let your legs precede you, pick up your feet as you step, stand up straight with your shoulders back, chin in, buttocks tucked under, tummy pulled taut. Let your arms swing freely, but not wildly. Try to be as relaxed as possible. That will be hard at first—but you'll soon get in the habit of walking properly and then you won't march along like a self-conscious soldier.

Exercises for a Graceful Walk

Do these exercises every day to help you have the muscle coordination for a fluid, relaxed gait. Our models have found them very helpful.

1. Lift right leg off the floor as high as you can, pointing toes directly in front of you. Keeping the knee stiff, swing the leg in an outward circle until it is directly behind you. Circle it back to starting point and repeat with left leg.

2. Lie down on your tummy. Rest head on your arms. Keeping legs together, stretch them straight out. Pull hip muscles down and together. Relax and repeat. At first there will be little muscle coordination, but keep it up—this is a good one.

3. Stand on left foot and swing right leg forward, leading with the knee. At the same time, swing left arm forward and right arm back. Then shift, swing right leg back and stretch it straight back as far as possible, while swinging left arm back and right arm forward. Repeat with left leg.

4. Stand with toes pointing straight ahead. With weight on the balls of your feet, lift one foot from the hip joint (*not* from the ankle or knee), and take a step the length of your foot. Walk forward along an imaginary straight line, touching the line with the inside of each heel as you put your feet down. Tuck hips under, which places the pelvis in the correct position. This also helps to straighten out the *S* curve if you are slightly swaybacked.

The Art of Sitting

Now for the art of sitting pretty. It's important for you, as well as our models, to know how to sit gracefully. Nervous? Then you'll be shifting from side to side, crossing and uncrossing your legs, twisting a handkerchief, or twirling a lock of hair. Poised? Here's how to do it:

1. Sit back in the seat and not on the edge of the chair.
2. Keep chest high, diaphragm flat.
3. Sit on your pelvic bones and not on the end of your spine.

When you approach a chair, do not throw yourself down into it as if you couldn't go another step. Walk up casually, turn your body slowly so that your back is toward the chair with the calf of your leg just touching the edge. With one foot slightly in front of the other, lower yourself slowly by bending your knees, but keeping your body erect. Do not lead with the fanny! Sink down, sitting at an angle, with knees to the right or left, whichever is more comfortable. Keep your knees together, not spread-eagle. Some women have difficulty doing this because of the excess

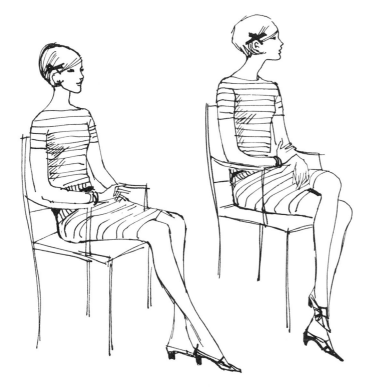

fat on their inner thighs, but if you have followed my instructions on exercise and diet, this, of course, won't happen to you!

Your ankles should be close together—perhaps an inch or so apart—with one foot in back and slightly to the side of the other. Never push your feet under the chair. If you must cross your legs, place the knee of one leg above the kneecap of the other—this gives a prettier angle. See that the toes of the upper leg are close to the ankle of the under leg. Now straighten your body with rib cage away from the hipbone. And, if you will keep your elbows away from your waist, your middle will appear much slimmer.

Getting out of a chair should be done gracefully, too. Place your weight on the ball of the back foot, slide to the edge of the chair, push on your feet while lifting yourself up. Lean forward, but keep your back as straight as possible. This will seem awkward at first, but practice does it, and in no time at all you will be doing it with the ease and smoothness of a Ford model.

13

The Ford Pamper Plan for Your Skin

Now that you've started on a brand-new figure, let's start on a brand-new face, too. The first consideration is the condition of your skin. Naturally, you'll never see a model with poor skin—she wouldn't last in her profession for a minute. Though some girls have good skin without too much effort, most of our models have to work at it, just as anyone else does. They treat their skin as one of their most precious possessions—they must. Occasionally we have had to drop a model from our lists completely because she let her complexion go. More often, we have retired a girl temporarily while she put on an all-out campaign to improve it. There's never been a girl who couldn't do it if she wanted to, though sometimes a lot of work is needed.

Your skin is exactly what you make it, from the inside as well as the outside. It isn't just a thick layer of something covering your body. It contains millions of cells that are constantly being renewed. It contains blood vessels, lymphatics, nerves, fatty tissues, oil glands, and sweat glands. It's a very complex structure that must be treated carefully if it is to be at its best.

Let me explain, briefly, what your skin is, and how it functions. There are two layers. The outer layer is called the epidermis, and it is the cellular part. The outermost part of the epidermis is composed of horny cells that age and die daily. Unless the dead cells are removed every day, they can form a hard layer of dead scale that gives a dull, leathery appearance.

The lower layer, the dermis, contains the blood vessels and most of the nerve endings. The dermis nourishes the outer layer and contains sweat glands and oil glands whose secretions reach the skin surface via pores seen in the epidermis. The sweat glands give off the waste and water, the oil glands produce lubricating oils that keep skin soft and pliable.

Below the dermis is the subcutaneous tissue, which is a layer of fatty tissue. This acts as a cushion to protect the nerves, glands, and blood vessels of the other two layers. This is the tissue that gives skin its support and contour. When this thins, the skin starts to loosen. The sagging is increased by the thinning and stretching of the dermis.

Skin performs many amazing functions, which you may not realize as you gaze at yourself in the mirror. Skin is a protective covering for the body, guarding it from injury and infection. It is a thermostat that helps regulate your body temperature. For instance, when you are too warm, it cools you through perspiration—when your sweat glands work overtime,

115

your body loses heat. When you are cold, the blood vessels in the skin contract to conserve the heat inside the body; when you are hot, they dilate. Skin can absorb, and doctors rely heavily on this ability. If it didn't, all the ointments in the world wouldn't be able to penetrate this surface—this is the basis on which the beauty creams work. The skin throws off waste from the body through the pores. And the skin breathes.

All of this marvelous activity goes on, of course, without our being aware of it. This is fine except that, instead of appreciating its miracles, we too often neglect and abuse our skins. Cosmetics can disguise imperfections; can, in fact, plaster over them; but they won't eliminate the imperfections and may compound them if not used correctly. Take care of your skin.

There are many factors that affect the condition and beauty of the skin. The most important is general health. You must have noticed that, when you are ill, it shows in your complexion, which becomes pasty, gray, or blemished. To a lesser degree, if you are not really sick but your health is not at its peak or you are run-down or afflicted with minor ailments, it shows in your skin, too. For many reasons—including your appearance—have a medical checkup if you have reason to suspect anything is wrong.

Your diet has a great deal to do with the condition of your skin. One reason our models have such good skin is because I have taught them to eat correctly. A poor diet will just about guarantee you a poor complexion. Sweets, rich pastries, fried and oily foods, soft drinks, all may play havoc. A lack of protein or the right vegetables and a certain amount of fat can promote skin problems. Remember that you can diet yourself to the proper weight and size, but you can also diet yourself into poor health—and a correlating appearance. Be sure to eat the proper foods. You'll find the Ford Model Diet contains all the nutritional elements you need.

An excess of liquor is another road to poor skin because it dehydrates and coarsens even the finest skin in almost no time at all. One of New York's most famous plastic surgeons once told me, "Alcohol ages the skin more quickly than anything I know except sun." Remember how you've felt after a night of particularly heavy drinking? Besides a hangover, you had a terrible thirst and your skin felt dry and leathery. That's because of the dehydration caused by the alcohol.

After food and drink, a great factor involved in your skin condition is the amount of sleep you get. If you continually shortchange yourself on sleep, your face will soon show it. One of the most beautiful women in the world, an actress who is about sixty-five now, never gets less than ten hours a night, and insists that this is her most vital beauty secret. Sleep is the time when your whole body, including your skin, revives itself. You can't make up for lost time, either. When I found out that one of our top models had been averaging five hours of sleep a night and trying to compensate by sleeping away her Sundays, I knew why her skin had lost its glow and vitality and why she had trouble getting through a model's long working day. When I talked to her about it, she promised to mend her ways—and she did. That's why she's still one of our top moneymaking models.

Until a few years ago, a dark, dark suntan was considered a status symbol as well as a thing of beauty. Now we know that too much tanning can turn your skin into leather, producing wrinkles and lines long before they're due, especially if you have dry skin. Some doctors consider it the one factor that will age your skin the fastest. There's no need to be brown as a berry anyway—stick with a light tan, acquired very, very slowly, with absolutely no burning. If you must be in the sun an excessive amount of time, get your light tan and then use one of those marvelous new sun-screening creams—all over your face and neck, and don't forget your arms, hands, and legs. Wear a brimmed hat or sunglasses to prevent deep squint lines from forming around your eyes. These are hard to get rid of. When you come back indoors, cream your face, if your skin is dry, or apply a good amount of moisturizer.

Even if your skin is in good condition, you must take proper care of it if you want to keep it that way. I'm going to tell you the way our models care for their miraculous outer layer. If you follow their example, you'll see immediate results—and, years from now, you'll really appreciate the efforts you've made. It's possible for a young girl to have

117

beautiful skin without lifting a finger to help it along, but she won't have it later if she doesn't work at it now.

There are three different types of skin: normal, dry, and oily. Normal skin produces just the right amount of oil. Dry skin has sebaceous glands that are not furnishing sufficient lubrication and moisture. The outer layer loses its intact smooth character. It tends to develop lines and wrinkles more quickly than other skins and needs more attention. And watch it, even if yours is normal now—everyone's skin tends to become more and more dry as the years go by.

Oily skin secretes more oil than is needed. The important thing is to keep it as cleansed of this excess oil as possible. Otherwise, your clogged pores can turn into blackheads, blemishes, and enlarged pores.

Some people have "combination" skin—that is, partly oily, partly dry. The oily sections are right down the center—the forehead, the nose, and the chin. The oily and dry sections must each be treated differently.

First, let's discuss my pamper plan for normal skin (then we'll talk about the specific problems and treatments for dry and oily skin). If you follow the plan for a month, I promise that the complexion you've always wanted will be yours. The results are not instantaneous, but at the end of thirty days you'll be thrilled with the improvement. And if you continue the pampering for another month, the change will be dramatic. You'll never slip back again. The first step of the pamper plan is to keep the skin fastidiously clean—there is no such thing as a beautiful, dirty skin. Before you start, bind your hair back from your face with a kerchief so that you can work right up to the hairline.

Nightly Skin Care

1. Cleanse your face with cleanser to remove every trace of makeup and grime.

2. Steam your face for ten minutes—every night for the first week and then twice weekly—with a hot cloth. Or sit in front of the sink, drape a towel over your head and the basin, and turn on the hot water, letting the vapor thoroughly steam your face. Those marvelous facial saunas are the easiest, so get one if you can.

3. Now make a rich lather of mild soap with your fingertips. Work gently into your skin with a circular and upward motion, starting at the chin and working upward toward the forehead. Give particular attention to the oil zone down the center of the face—forehead, nose, chin. And be particularly gentle in the area of the eyes.

4. Rinse with cool water, no less than twenty times, using your cupped hands.

5. Blot dry with a Turkish towel. Never rub or pull the skin.

6. Apply a mild freshening lotion. Never use a harsh astringent, no matter what your skin type is.

7. Apply moisturizer. This is important even if you have oily skin—oil and moisture are not the same, and it is essential to replace moisture constantly. Leave it on until you cleanse again.

119

Morning Skin Care

1. Cleanse face again with the same fingertip washing that you used at night.
2. Rinse thoroughly.
3. Blot dry.
4. Apply moisturizer.
5. Apply makeup, even if you are doing nothing in particular—it acts as a protective shield against the elements and the dirt in the air.

For dry or oily skins, you must vary the pamper plan a bit. Let's consider dry skin first.

Dry Skin

It's impossible to replace oils in the skin as you can't penetrate it that deeply. However, moisture can and must be replaced. Use moisturizer morning, noon, and night. Use lubricants after your skin has been well hydrated—this keeps the water in the skin. Steam your face once a week. Dry skin should be cleansed with a cream or lotion cleanser every day. Use soap only once a week. Follow by a freshener applied to a cotton pad that has been soaked in water and wrung out. When you cleanse, be very gentle with dry skin—use only your fingertips, or the softest cloth. Occasionally, give your face and neck a gentle massage with mineral oil or peanut oil to lubricate the surface of the skin and soften little lines. Never use a cake or matte makeup for dry skin, but rather a liquid foundation. And always wear it over your moisturizer. Be wary of the sun—it is dry skin's worst enemy.

Oily Skin

Cleansing is the vital thing for oily skin to keep the pores from getting clogged. Clogged pores cause blackheads and troubled skin. Steaming is particularly important and, in extreme cases, should be done twice a day until the skin is clear. Use a plain mild soap twice a day—or more if you can manage it. (One dermatologist I know recommends washing six times a day.) Instead of fingertips, wash with a nubbly washcloth and be particularly vigorous around the nose and chin sections. Between times, if your makeup turns oily, blot with pads made for this purpose, or splash cool water on your face (or dab on with wet cotton), and press dry with a towel or tissue. Don't go in for sun treatments, harsh cleansers, medicated makeups, and astringents. These will only dry the surface of the skin and cause it to flake. And it might well cause it to produce *more* oil to compensate for the loss. Stay away from creams, except for moisturizers.

If you have blackheads, steam your face thoroughly before you work on them. Then *gently* squeeze with your fingertips and a tissue. Do not insist if blackheads don't pop out immediately, but steam your face again and try once more. If nothing happens with a gentle squeeze, forget it. If you attack these little monsters too vigorously, you can turn them into worse problems. If you have pimples that are topped with whiteheads, sterilize a needle by passing through a flame and gently prick the white section. Press with a tissue—or squeeze *very* gently—until only clear blood comes out. Then dab on antiseptic, alcohol, or witch hazel. If you have acne, follow my oily skin program religiously. Sleep as much as possible, try not to get upset, and watch your diet!

If you have oily skin without acne, watch what you eat, too. Oily, fatty foods can show up in your face—stay away from nuts, fried foods, chocolate, gravy, and seafoods. The new face steamers make it possible to care for disturbed skin as never before. Mobilize yourself and attack your problem with vigor. You *can* cure your skin problems yourself.

Combination Skin

Treat the dry parts as dry skin and the oily parts as oily skin. This makes life a little more difficult but it's no real problem. Keep cream away from the forehead, nose, and chin where your face is oily. Apply it to the eye area, the cheeks, jaws, neck, and throat.

Now you'll never be able to completely prevent lines and wrinkles in your face when you hit middle-age, and there's not much point in

1

2

worrying about it. But you can keep them to a minimum by treating your skin kindly from teen-age on. Even if you've been neglecting it for years until this moment, it's not too late to start. Everything you do for it will help. Remember sun is the great ager.

One way to keep skin in good condition, supple and elastic, is to exercise it. Every week or so, give yourself a facial massage to stimulate the circulation and tone up the underlying muscles. With a small amount of cream on your fingertips, gently work it into your face, always with an upward and circular motion. Be particularly gentle around the eyes. Then give your face little slaps all over. Cleanse thoroughly.

The other way to move your face is to do facial exercises. Here are some to do whenever you happen to think of it. They are really a lot of fun especially if you watch yourself in the mirror. But don't do them in front of anyone—he'll think you've gone mad.

Facial Exercises

1. Open your mouth wide, dropping your jaw down as far as possible. Then snap your lips together quickly. Repeat several times.

2. Puff your cheeks out like apples and blow to the right, then to the left, without moving your head.

3. Exercise your jaws with a chewing-gum motion, or get a real stick of sugarless gum and chew madly.

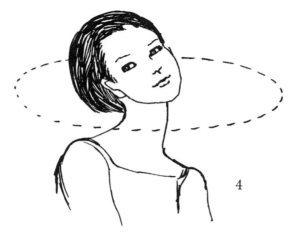

4

4. Roll your head around in as full a circle as you can manage, stretching your neck as you go.

5. Throw your head back as far as you can, then return to normal position with eyes peering straight ahead.

6. First purse your mouth; then with mouth open, make the motions of chewing vigorously. Alternate briskly.

7. Puff out cheeks, then puff hard against the cheeks and upper lip. Blow through slightly open lips, as though you were tooting a horn.

8. Chew gum and try to whistle at the same time, keeping the gum toward the front of your mouth. This is good for those thin lines between the nose and the corners of the mouth.

9. Stick your tongue out as far as you can and try to touch the tip of your nose. You'll find it helps a flabby chin line.

Do these exercises about twenty-five times each as often as you can manage, but at least every day. And try to keep from making facial expressions that produce unattractive lines, such as raising eyebrows, frowning, scowling, pursing the lips. Do these long enough and constantly enough, and you'll find your face permanently creased. F., one of our top models, finally had to find another profession because she developed a series of horizontal lines across her forehead from constantly raising her eyebrows. Control your facial expressions, and you'll control the aging process a bit.

The big point to remember is that skin care is an everyday affair. Guard your skin like gold, and you'll see the results.

14

Makeup–Accentuating the Positive

Makeup is the art of making the most of what you've got. It can enhance the most beautiful face and make marvelous changes in the most plain. Probably the top artists in the field of makeup today are the professional models who have made a business of perfecting their own beauty for the world to see. Even actresses don't know as much about it as the models do—their makeup is applied by a professional while they lie back and relax. A model must learn to apply her own, many times a day for the different photographic situations with which she must work. And she must be fast and deft, completely sure of herself, as there's never much time to lose. You can do the same thing, but you'll have to learn how to do it, just as the models do. And that takes practice.

Once you know which features you want to accent and which you want to hide, the rest is easy. The most important rule to remember is to keep your makeup natural. Except perhaps for eye makeup, if it's obvious, it's wrong. Makeup is intended to play up your beauty, not to cover you like a mask. Makeup should never look heavy or painted. True, if you see a model on the street or in the studio, you might think she's overdone it, but remember that models must often exaggerate for the camera. *You* shouldn't.

Our models start by learning about makeup from me. I teach them all the basics and a few tricks besides. Few of our girls are so perfect that they need absolutely no help from cosmetics, and you can learn from them. You can enlarge your eyes, diminish your nose, give shape to a shapeless mouth. With the right makeup, the world is yours.

All our models have to learn how to use cosmetics and the tools needed to apply them. They have to practice, practice, practice. No one can use a lip liner perfectly, for example, until she's tried many, many times. Set aside ten or fifteen minutes a day for your makeup practice— just at first. Don't try to learn more than one procedure at a time, or you'll just get confused. Practice until you've mastered one trick, then go on to another. At first your hand will be wobbly, and the lines may not be at all where you wish them to be. But soon the whole thing will be as natural and automatic as writing your name. It's my experience that, after ten days, perfection in applying makeup starts to set in in spite of yourself.

Be sure you have a comfortable place to work and, most particularly, a good natural light. You must be able to see yourself as you'll look *outdoors* with the sun shining. Invest in just the basic cosmetics—you can always try out others later. Always apply makeup to a clean face, never

on top of old makeup or a dirty face. Always remove every trace of it before you go to bed. Keep your powder puffs and sponges and brushes immaculately clean, or you'll be applying dirt and old caked makeup to your clean face.

Before you begin, clean your skin thoroughly and apply moisturizer. Allow it to set for a few seconds. Ready? Let's go.

Foundation

1. Apply liquid makeup base in a near skin tone evenly all over your face up to the hairline, out to the ears, and blend over your neck. (I prefer liquid foundation because we have found that it blends more easily than other types and offers excellent opportunities for improving on the bone structure. I feel that cake makeup highlights lines, may dry the skin, and gives an unnatural look.)

2. Look in the mirror and suck in your cheeks. Relax. Apply a *slightly* darker makeup in the area that was pulled in. Blend it carefully

and extend it out to your ears so that the difference in shades is not discernible. This gives the face a more hollow-cheeked look. (To look even more hollow-cheeked, if your face is very full, apply dry shadow with a brush over your powder later on.)

3. Apply lighter makeup in the area under your eyes, blending it carefully into the base. This hides shadows and circles. Make sure it is a creamy makeup so that it doesn't dry the delicate skin.

4. Apply loose powder with a clean puff or a wad of cotton. Be sure it is the same color as your base or a no-color finishing powder and that it covers the entire face. Dust away the excess.

5. I believe in facial color applied with a brush. Now is the time to add whatever color you may need. To be honest with you, I don't like rouge very much—it tends to look artificial, unless you use the beige shades that are never too pink. But if you must wear it, blend it, blend it, blend it, so that it looks like it's part of you. Smile and apply it on your puffed-out cheeks, never below the nose, and carry it on up and out right into the hairline below the temples. The idea is to look like those healthy cheeks are yours.

Camouflage

Now your basic face is on (we'll get to eyes and lips later). But there are lots of little tricks we've developed to camouflage imperfections. The whole secret of facial contouring is simple—lighter makeup emphasizes, darker makeup minimizes. Therefore, you will apply lighter makeup to whatever features you want to accent or enlarge and darker to whatever you want to diminish. *Always apply it over your base,* blend them carefully together, and set with powder.

1. If your nose is too broad, draw a thin line of makeup (in a shade lighter than your base) down the center of your nose over your base. Then blend a shade darker makeup along the sides of the nose. Blend carefully and powder. The narrowness of the nose will depend on how high on your nose you apply the darker shadow—the higher the narrower.

2. To shorten a long nose, apply a darker shade of makeup under the tip.

3. To narrow a wide jawline, carefully blend a darker shade over the part of the jawline you wish to minimize.

4. To lower a very high forehead, apply a darker shade along the hairline. You can even use two shades, one darker than the other, making sure the darkest is next to the hairline.

5. To raise a low forehead, apply a lighter shade along the hairline.

6. To thin down a very full face, apply white makeup just along the cheekbone. Then take your darker makeup and make a triangle just under the cheekbone, its apex pointing down, the base beginning just under the cheekbone. Apply this over your regular base. For an oval look, use a second darker shade and blend it from the ears to the chin

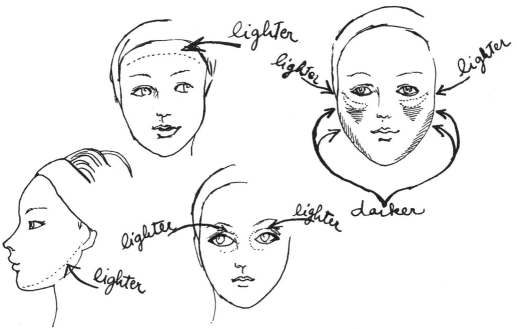

along the jawline. It should be about an inch wide at the ears and taper down to a hairline at the chin. This goes over your regular base. Powder, and dust a tiny bit of face shadow in this area for emphasis. Again, remember to be *subtle*—the shading should never be noticeable.

7. To correct a receding chin line, make a light outline of lighter makeup from your ears down along the edge of the jawline to your chin. Now take the darker makeup and apply it within the light frame.

8. To widen your eyes, apply lighter makeup on the inner eyelids and on the sides of your nose next to the eyes and start your eyeline in the middle of the upper lid.

Got the idea? You can make an amazing difference in the shape of your face if you know how to do it—and now you do.

Eye Makeup

Before I start giving you the models' tricks with eyes, be sure you are using a really good light and a mirror you can get close to. You'll need powder, tweezers, an eyebrow brush, a sharp black eye liner pencil or the cake type with a brush, an eyebrow pencil that closely matches the

color of your own brows, a charcoal-gray eye liner, and black mascara. And you'll need brown eye shadow and creamy-white eye makeup.

Look at your eyes in the mirror to learn your problems. Everyone needs eye makeup, even our most beautiful models. Every single one of them wears eye makeup during every single waking hour. If they didn't, I'm sure very few would be paid the fabulous fees they get for posing. Though models do exaggerate their eye makeup for the camera, they don't overdo it like some of the girls you see on the street—the idea is *not* to look like a clown who hasn't had enough sleep.

Eye makeup is no longer just for models or actresses or gaudy girls—it's for everybody; and if you don't wear it, you'll look washed out and drab today. It's just as important as lipstick—and you know you wouldn't want to be seen without that (unless you're under seventeen) .

EYE SHADOW

First, eye shadow. If you want a color, choose one that compliments the color of your eyes and blends with your clothing. Muted shades are always best for daytime, and our models prefer the browns, grays, mushroom shades, and white to the more vivid colors, which really are better for the evening hours.

For daytime, put a line of shadow on the upper lid, blending with your forefinger or brush in a wide line as close as possible to the lashes. Blend it up, down, and to either side, to cover the whole lid up to the crease. You can extend it out a bit beyond your eyes to make them look larger. The shadow must never look patchy or heavy. Now powder lightly to set the shadow (pressing it on rather than rubbing) and dust away the excess with a tissue. Now you can, if you wish, apply a little more shadow if you want the color more definite. For a heavy-lidded

130

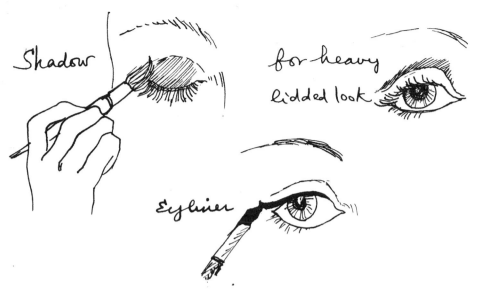

look, apply a brown or gray line with a brush, in an arch, along the crease.

EYE LINER

Apply your eye liner as close to your lash roots as possible. You do this by drawing a line from the inner edge of the upper lid out to the outer corner, making the line a little wider as you go out. If your hand seems shaky at first, that's quite natural. Don't worry, by the end of a week, if you practice every day, it will seem very simple. Some of our models draw the line right through the root of their own lashes so that there is no space at all. Choose your weapon—use a black pencil, well-sharpened, or a brush and cream, or cake liner. Fashion models always use black, but you may not want so much emphasis. If so, choose brown or dark gray. Don't make the line too heavy; start with a very thin line at the inner corner and let it widen just a bit as you get toward the outer edge. Don't draw the line close to the very end of your eye, but a quarter-inch from the end start a slight upward curve. Never extend it beyond the crease of the eye.

Now take the liner and make a very, very thin line just under the outer corner of the lashes and extended out a bit. And you can, with a very fine brush, draw on some tiny lower lashes.

131

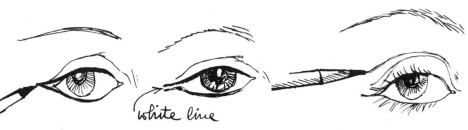

white line

Tricks with eye liners: You can change the shape and spacing of your eyes to a considerable extent with the use of lines and shades of makeup.

To enlarge your eyes: take your black liner and outline your top lid, extending the eyeline a fraction, about a sixteenth of an inch, beyond the natural corner of your top lid. Now take a charcoal gray or brown eye liner—or brown eye shadow and brush—and draw a line along the lower lid, starting about a quarter-inch from the outer corner, and extend it out until it meets the black line, forming a tiny triangle. Fill in the triangle with white eye makeup applied with a brush.

Another way to make your eyes look larger, suggested one of our most successful girls, is to make a tiny line of white eye makeup at the outer corners. Then draw your upper eyeline, extending it outward about a sixteenth of an inch. With the charcoal or brown eye liner, draw a line starting just inside the outer corner of the lower lid and extend straight out parallel with the two other lines. Draw the lines softly and subtly, and no one will know that your eyes are anything smaller than saucers.

A third trick to make small eyes seem much larger and large eyes positively enormous: draw a thin brown line under the brow just under the bone. Once drawn, the line is almost erased, with just a hint remaining. This time the originator wasn't one of my models—it was Greta Garbo.

If your eyelids are too heavy, use a darker shade of makeup on the lids over your regular shade. Then use white or a light shade of makeup under your brow above the crease.

If your eyes are too deep-set, use light eye makeup on the eyelid above a narrow line of eye shadow. Then apply darker makeup on the area above the crease and under the brow. Blend carefully. Almost every model uses this trick. If your eyes are extremely deep-set, apply mascara only to the _ends_ of the lashes.

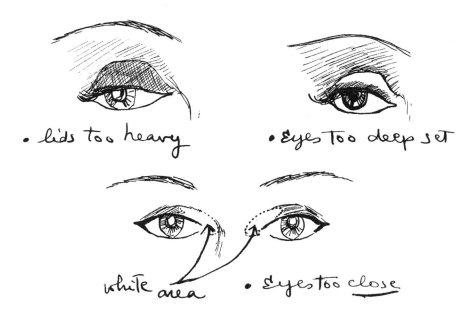

• lids too heavy   • Eyes Too deep set

white area   • Eyes too close

For eyes that are too close together, apply white eye makeup between your nose and the inner corners of your eyes. Then blend a little a fraction of an inch along your upper lid. Start your eye shadow, eye liner and mascara only along the outer half of your eye, extending it outward.

EYEBROWS

Always choose an eyebrow pencil in a shade that closely matches your hair. It may be a slightly intensified tone, but *never, never* use a black pencil. If you are a brunet, dark brown is your eyebrow pencil color. Brownettes, from medium to light, should use one of the paler brown shades. There are reddish pencils for redheads and blonds look marvelous with pale brown flecked with gray. Try using a gold pencil for highlights in red brows and an auburn color in very dark brows.

Do not draw just one line and call it an eyebrow. Use light short strokes, as if you were creating each new hair, and keep the look perfectly natural. Start on the end nearest the center and work out. If you need a slight arch on the upper side, draw it hair by hair. Any other shaping should be done with tweezers, except for lengthening if your brows are too short. Some models draw against the grain—try it and see if this is easier for you.

It is vital never to distort your brows: they should be as individual

133

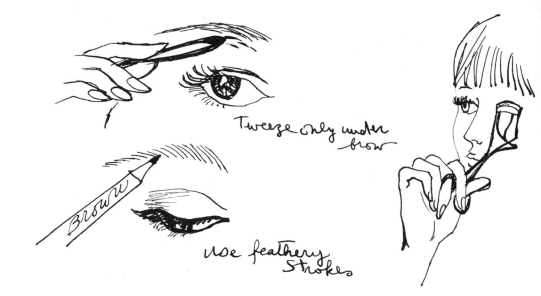

Tweeze only under brow

Brown

use feathery strokes

as the shape of your face, and they should never be too thin or artificial. Most brows need only a little tweezing and then only for shape. The natural look is the fashion look today.

Before you pluck your eyebrows, brush them up and then sideways. This should show you their true natural shape. Apply a little cream to the area. Pluck out any straggly hairs between the brows—the brows should start at the inner corners of your eyes. Then pluck out any stray hairs beneath. If they need a slight arching, pluck from below only. Go slowly and don't go overboard. You must leave most of your own eyebrows—just pluck enough to produce a shape.

The best way to decide how to correct your brows is to apply makeup base over them. Then, staring in the mirror, experiment by drawing a few different shapes with your eyebrow pencil. Do only one brow at a time, so you can see the difference.

Tricks with eyebrows: Small eyes: make your brows a little thicker by building them up just a bit on top to emphasize them. Clear out straggly hairs underneath, and arch them slightly in the outer third to give more space.

Deep-set eyes: again enlarge the space between the eyes and brows—raise the brows slightly by penciling in a little above the bone.

Eyes too close together: widen the space between the brows a little by plucking, and extend the pencil line at the ends.

Eyes too far apart: pencil eyebrows a little closer to the nose, and do not extend them out at the ends.

Bulging eyes: tweeze out any hairs that grow down too far over your eyes and raise the brows slightly from below.

EYELASHES

Eyelashes do not grow in a straight line, but in two or three irregular rows, growing more heavily in the center of the lid. A lash reaches its full length in about ten weeks, and each one lives from three to five months. Like the hairs on your head, there is nothing you can do directly to stimulate growth. It's wishful thinking to try gently pulling them or applying petroleum jelly—it doesn't help. All you can do is enhance what you've got. If you're lucky, you'll have your own long silky lashes. If you're not, you can dress up what you've got with mascara or fake lashes.

First, arm yourself with an eyelash curler. When the lashes are straight, they tend to curtain the eyes and make them look smaller. When they are swept upward, more of the iris is revealed and they seem larger and more luminous. To achieve this wide-eyed effect takes exactly thirty seconds. Grip the hairs gently with the curler, count up to thirty, and release. For a more pronounced curl, release the grip and move to a new position two or three times. Another reason this is a good idea is to keep the lashes from brushing against the lenses of your eyeglasses if you wear them.

MASCARA

Choose the type of mascara you like best—cream, cake, waterproof, or otherwise. Whatever you choose, get any color as long as it's *black*. The only exception to this rule is if you have absolutely white brows and lashes; then choose brown. Be sure your eye liner is on perfectly before you start with the mascara.

With a brush or wand, apply the mascara with upward and outward strokes. Don't use too much or your lashes will become matted. Now

lightly pat on loose power or apply lash builder. Then mascara again. If you want to be really dramatic, you can repeat this a couple more times. You'll be astounded at the new "growth" you've produced.

If your lower lashes are quite full, apply mascara lightly here, too. If they are skimpy, the mascara will only point that up, so draw them in as I've mentioned above, using a brown shade.

FALSE EYELASHES

Fake lashes, not too long ago, were seen only on actresses or models, but now everybody realizes they're great. They require a lot of practice in handling, but once you have the knack, they're easy to put on.

Most models prefer the English lashes and wear one, two, or three pairs, depending on the effect they want. They usually cut their own, but I think the nonprofessional should probably buy the precut lashes—it's quite an art to feather the lashes perfectly. They should not go from corner to corner of the eye, but start about an eighth of an inch from the inner corner and end just at the end of your own natural lashes. They should be shorter toward the inner edge and longer toward the outer. Don't wear them too long or too thick or too bluntly cut, they'll look too

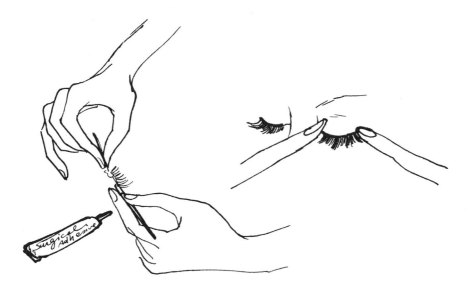

fake—and that's not the idea. You should look like you've got your *own* long, silky lashes. I recommend buying a medium-expensive variety. They wear well, and some really are overpriced. Four to six dollars is ample to spend on eyelashes. But while you're learning how to put them on, buy a cheap pair with which to practice.

Here's how to apply them. First put on all your eye makeup except mascara, including eye liner (a nongreasy kind, perhaps the cake type). Hold the lashes with tweezers and, with a pin or a toothpick, apply the surgical adhesive in a *very thin* line along the base. Place the lashes as close as possible to the roots of your own, pressing down with your finger, the tweezers, or the handle of an eyeline brush. There should be no space between the two sets. If necessary, use mascara to stick the two sets together. Most models don't use mascara on the false lashes, but only on their own. Remove at bedtime by pulling off gently. Wash carefully with warm water and dry gently over your finger with a towel or tissue. Clean off adhesive with special remover every so often, or dip the whole set in a solution made for the purpose. I know it's tough to learn how to put false lashes on expertly, but once you do, you'll feel naked without them.

Now your makeup's complete. Just flick the brows and lashes with an eyebrow brush, and you are ready to face the world.

Remember always to remove your mascara—along with all your other makeup—at night. Use an oily remover or special pads you can buy at any cosmetic counter. If you let mascara build up, your lashes may

become dry and brittle. If you've run out of special cleanser, use peanut or mineral oil.

If your eyes aren't healthy and sparkling, no amount of makeup will disguise it. Your eyes reflect your general condition—you must be in good physical shape, eat properly, get enough sleep. Have your eyes checked to be sure you don't need correction. If you don't like glasses, you can get contact lenses, but, in any case, don't ruin your sight by letting vanity stand in your way. Besides it's better to wear glasses than to squint or to pass your best friend on the street without knowing it. Some of our most successful models, girls you've seen looking out from the fashion magazines with that wide-eyed look, are so nearsighted they can't sign a release form without reaching for their glasses.

A word on sunglasses: never buy cheap sunglasses. The lenses should be ground, polished, and curved. And never wear them at night or indoors, but only when the sunlight is so bright that it interferes with your sight.

If your eyes are tired, they'll look it—they'll be lackluster and perhaps even bloodshot and droopy. Are you getting enough sleep? If your eyes feel tired during the day, lie down and take a nap or at least close your eyes for a while, perhaps with refreshing eye pads. Soak pads of cotton in witch hazel or a mild solution of boric acid. Lie down for fifteen minutes. Freshen the pads as they become warm.

Try to avoid glare—bright sunlight, snow, sand, or water, shiny walls, light shining directly into the eyes, a too-bright reading bulb, glazed paper, etc. But be sure you have *enough* soft light for what you are doing.

Here are ways I recommend to our girls for relieving mild eyestrain or weariness.

1. Cover your eyes with your cupped hands. Think of black velvet.

2. Blink quickly ten times, then close your eyes for several seconds. Repeat.

3. Open your eyes as wide as possible, then shut them tight. Try to do this without moving your brows.

4. When doing close work, look up frequently, focusing your eyes on an object as far away as possible.

5. Press your index finger against the center of your forehead and hold for a minute to relax eye and forehead muscles.

You can do the above routines at your desk or in public. The following are probably best done in privacy:

1. Hold your index finger in front of you at eye level, about a foot from your face. Focus on it. Then, while moving your finger slowly to your nose, look to the right, back to the finger, then to the left, and back to the finger. Repeat, looking up and down.

2. Without turning your head, roll your eyes slowly toward the right, then to the left. Then roll them up, then down.

139

CROW'S-FEET

Lines and wrinkles around the eyes, or crow's-feet, are the bane of many women's existence. The skin in this area is very thin and sensitive, because there is no guarding bone structure and no oil glands. Eye creams don't really help as it is moisture that is needed. Moisturizer is utterly essential night and day. And try a little peanut oil to help soften the lines a bit.

Lip Makeup

After all the rest of your makeup is on perfectly, it is time to put on your lip makeup, and this is an important step. After your eyes, your mouth is noticed first. A mouth can be mobile, expressive, inviting, or it can be a slash of color, a blurred smudge. The shape of your mouth, if it isn't perfect already, can be changed to a considerable extent. Keep in mind that your lips should be curved and fairly full, and that you'll look more appealing with the corners of your mouth turned up just slightly. Any correction you do to your lips, however, should look as natural as possible. I'll tell you how our models do it. But first, here's the way they apply their lip makeup.

Remove all traces of old color on your lips. Now lightly powder your lips, and dust away any excess. This will prevent the lipstick from smearing or running. Now take a sharp lip liner, and prop your elbow on a firm surface. Starting from a point just above the left corner of your

140

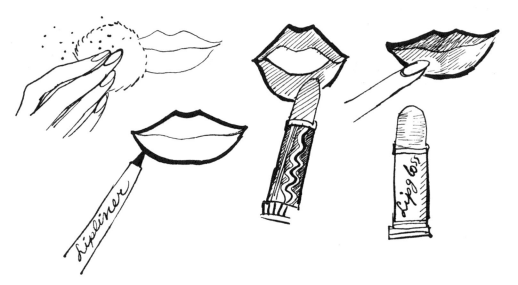

mouth, draw a line up to the left peak of the bow of your upper lip—in one smooth stroke. Then, from the right, draw the line to the right peak. Now join the peaks by following the natural bow of your lips. The line that joins the peaks should be straight or almost straight—cupid's bows are "out."

Now underline the middle two-thirds of the lower lip with a slightly curved line. Then draw in the remaining outer sections to the very corners of your mouth.

If you find this procedure difficult, remember that practice makes perfect. Use your practice time to outline your lips over and over again. Before long, you'll be sure and deft, and your hand won't shake!

Now you fill in the outline with lipstick. Use a brush or a tube, whichever you prefer.

Coat the lips lightly with lipsheen, which gives a moist, dewy look.

Simple?

PROBLEM LIPS

1. If your mouth is not long enough, try starting your left lip line slightly above and to the left of the corner. Then draw one short stroke from this line to the corner of your mouth. Do the same thing on the other side. The idea is to pretend that the far corners of the little lines

141

not long
Enough   too thin   too full   too full
lower lip

are the corners of your mouth. Now draw from the peaks to these corners, perhaps drawing slightly above the peaks to make them smoother. What you've done is to make an "almost triangle" from the peak of your upper lip to the extended corner, to the real corner of your upper lip. Then draw your lower lip.

2. To make a thin mouth look fuller, outline it with a darker shade just outside the natural edge of the lips. Fill in with a slightly lighter shade. Try adding a touch of white eye makeup in the very middle of your mouth where the lips join for an even fuller effect.

3. If your mouth is too full, first cover your mouth with makeup base, then powder, but make the base heavy enough to cover the outline of your lips. Now draw your lip line no more than a sixteenth of an inch inside the natural line.

4. For a lower lip that's too full, draw your lip liner just inside your natural lip line. Use a *slightly* darker shade of lipstick on this lip to make it look smaller or apply a beige gloss only to the top lip.

Remember, when using all of these models' tricks, not to be too obvious. Just the slightest amount of correction can do a lot for your appearance. Models can completely remodel their lips for the camera— but it isn't wise for streetwear.

As for the color of your lipsticks, that is such a personal affair that it is hard for me to generalize. Fashions in lip color change every season. However, you must remember that the color must blend not only with your hair color and skin tone, but with your clothes, your eye shadow, and your nail polish. Dark colors haven't been fashionable for a long time, so stay away from them (are you listening, you older ladies?) . Very light, almost white shades are risky for most of us, especially anyone over twenty-five. They have a tendency to make you look sick or washed out or old. For most women, the light, bright pastel shades are best. Iridescent lipsticks are fun, but keep them for nighttime and night lights.

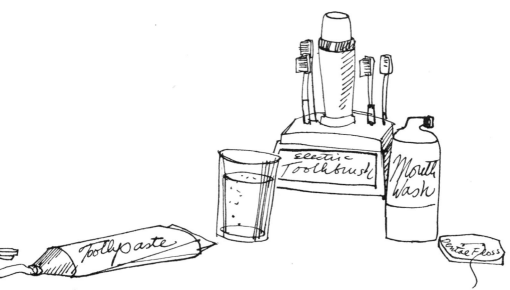

Before we leave the subject of mouths, let me talk a minute about teeth. No matter how beautifully you put on your makeup, the entire effect will be ruined if, when you open your lips to smile, your teeth are poor. Brush your teeth with an electric toothbrush at least twice a day and hopefully more often—after eating anything. Carry a little folding toothbrush in your handbag if you spend much time away from home. Use dental floss to get out the food that sneaks into the spaces between the teeth. Massage your gums every day, either with your fingers or with a Water Pik. More teeth are lost due to lack of gum care than are ever lost to cavities. Don't forget that twice yearly date with your dentist. Keep a firm grip on your diet—eat the foods that are healthy for you and stay away from sweets and soft drinks. Eat some vegetables raw to give your teeth a workout.

Get in the habit of using mouthwash. Buy a bottle or make your own by combining a half-teaspoon of salt with a half-glass of water, or a quarter-teaspoon of baking soda in a half-glass of water. You don't want to have what your best friend won't tell you about.

If your teeth are really unattractive because of past neglect or because they're crooked or yellow or poorly shaped, it's still possible to do something about them. At almost any age, you can have them straightened by a competent orthodontist. Or you can have them capped—just be sure that you know the work of the man you select if you're considering tooth capping.

143

15
Your Neck and
Your Shoulders

Your neckline needs skin care and cosmetic help if you don't want it to date you. It can, if you don't watch out. You can't see your neck without special effort when you look in the mirror, but it's in full view of every friend or foe. The neck is the continuation of the face, but many women seem to forget that. They'll go to any lengths to pamper their faces but don't pay attention to their throats where the skin often becomes crepey and wrinkled before any other part of the body. Even if your face is young and firm, a droopy neck will tattletale. Many a model has left the field because of this problem.

The time to start working on your neck is now, just as all of my models do if they're smart. If you are young, and this talk of wrinkles and droops seems way out of your realm, pay attention anyway. This is the moment to take preventive measures. If you already are having a neckline problem, much can be accomplished if you work at it. You must give your neck and shoulders good skin care; you must watch your posture, and you must exercise.

Neck

Like the area around your eyes, the skin on your neck has fewer oil glands than your face and, therefore, it tends to become dry and lined first. *You* must supply it with oil.

1. Using a moisturizing cream, start at the base of the throat. Massage upward with a rotary motion, following the muscle structure. Always massage upward, never pull down or stretch the skin. The force of gravity does enough damage without giving it any assistance.

2. Wrap a hot towel around your throat, reheating it several times as it cools. Follow this with heated skin freshener applied with a piece of cotton.

145

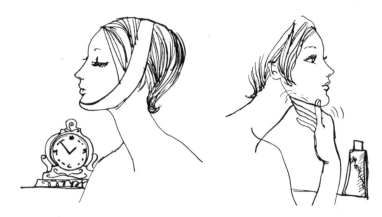

3. If you ever use a chin strap (and I think they do some good, though my special exercises are even better), perform this routine before you put it on. Thoroughly cleanse throat with a cream. Now apply a lubricating cream over the chin, jaw, and throat. Rub in gently. Place a pad of cotton soaked with skin freshener under the chin, on top of the cream. Then put on the chin strap and wear it for about twenty minutes.

4. Apply moisturizer (after cleansing if you've used the lubricating cream). Using the backs of your fingers, gently tap your chin from jawline to jawline. Now, with the fingers of your right hand, palm up, pat the left side of your throat from collarbone to jaw. Now use the left hand to do the same on the right side.

Perhaps you've noticed the way models—or actresses or other beautiful women—carry themselves. You, too, if you want to be beautiful, must work on your posture. It is especially important if you want to have a pretty neck. Learn to keep your head set straight on your shoulders, not slouched forward. Your head should be raised, with the tips of the ears above your shoulders. The neck should be the same length in front as it is in back. If you lower your chin, you'll see that your neck is shorter in front, longer in back, giving a hangdog look. Raise it so that the distances are even. This simple correction will take years off your appearance if you're past forty.

Keep in mind that the muscles that hold the head erect are also responsible for keeping the throat line firm. When the head is held high, the muscles remain taut. But if you slump, jutting your head forward, this stretches and slackens the muscles, both in the face and the throat.

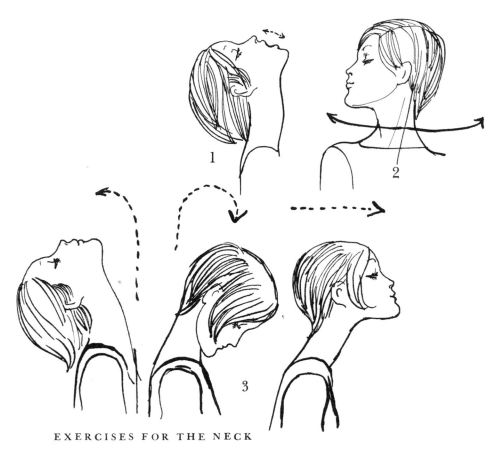

EXERCISES FOR THE NECK

Are you ready to do some work? Do these exercises whether you already have a neckline problem or not—they will help prevent drooping and wrinkling and they will help to correct an existing situation.

1. Stand straight, hands at sides. Throw your head back as far as possible until you feel the muscles pulling. Keeping head back, drop your chin. Now, open and close your mouth. Repeat several times.

2. Standing, turn chin to the right as far as you can, trying to carry your chin over your right shoulder. Thrust your chin up. Do several times on the right. Then repeat, turning to the left.

3. Thrust head back as far as possible, then drop it forward trying to touch chin to your chest. Straighten head and lift chin slightly and thrust it forward as though you are trying to push a heavy object out of the way.

147

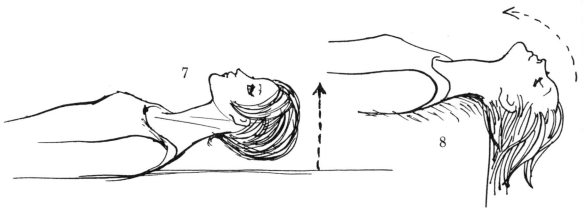

4. Bend to the floor, head down, and body relaxed. Remain in this position until you feel the blood rushing to your head. Now slowly stand up and pivot your head around slowly, first to one side and then the other.

5. With head thrown back, try to touch the tip of your tongue to the tip of your nose. You may have done this as a child, just to be naughty. Now you have a *real* reason for doing it!

6. Cup chin in the palm of your hand. Push hand up while trying to open mouth against the pressure.

7. Lie on the floor on your back. Raise your head very slowly off the floor, being certain to point your chin directly toward the ceiling. Then lower your head, SLOWLY, and relax.

8. You can be nice and comfortable when you do this exercise as it is to be done on your bed. Lie on your back, and let your head hang over the edge. Keep your shoulders on the bed. Slowly lift your head to bed level and then slowly lower. Repeat several times.

Need a little rest now? Give your neck a quick massage back of the ears for relaxation and stimulation. Massage gently in a rotary motion. Now back to work!

Shoulders

Just as your face leads down to your neck, your neck leads to your shoulders, and these must get a little attention, too. Posture is the main

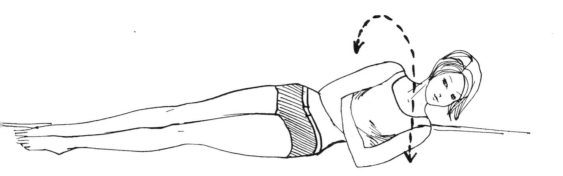

thing here—don't hump your shoulders forward or you will not only end up with a rounded back but a dowager's hump as well. Keep your shoulders back, and *relax* them, letting your arms hang naturally at your sides. If your shoulders are back, your neck will usually straighten up with it and so will your back.

The skin on your shoulders should glow. All skin needs stimulation and your shoulders need the same consideration you give your face and neck. Here's what our models do to stimulate the circulation of the shoulders and to keep the skin luminous.

First, cleanse with warm water and rich soapsuds when you bathe. Now use a stiff bath brush to scrub away the dead scales and grit. Rinse well and pat dry. Apply a cleansing cream all over your shoulders. Remove cream with tissues. Take a large fluffy towel, wring it out in hot water, place on your shoulders, and press against the skin. Do this several times, and your skin should be rosy and glowing. While the skin is warm, apply moisturizer, rubbing it into the little hollows at the side of your neck right above the collarbone. Massage the shoulders, around the base of the neck, and down over the top of your chest. Remove excess moisturizer and rub a cotton-covered ice cube over the skin.

EXERCISES FOR THE SHOULDERS

1. Lie on your back on the floor. With arms folded across your chest, twist your upper body from side to side, touching the floor. This will help roll off some of that accumulated shoulder fat, especially where the flesh tends to be flabby at the outsides of your shoulder blades.

2. Sit on the floor with your back against the wall, legs out in front of you and slightly bent. Keep feet flat on the floor. Clasp underarms just below the elbow, arms at shoulder level. Now, with the small of the back and your head touching the wall, try to bring your arms up overhead until the elbows touch the wall. Do this several times, pushing the arms up as hard as you can.

This one is good for shoulders and that dowager's hump.

3. Sit on the floor with your back against the wall. Relax, dropping your head forward on your chest. Slowly roll your spine up the wall, then push the back of your neck tight back on the wall and hold it while you count to ten.

16
Hair–
Your Crowning Glory

There's a lot more to hair care than finding the most attractive style for you. If you really want your hair to be your crowning glory, and it can be, your hair must be healthy and clean as well as nicely arranged. Hair is made up of the same protein material that forms your fingernails and toenails. The proper diet, sufficient sleep, exercise, and

plenty of water help keep all three in good health. Like your skin, your hair gives away a lot of secrets: it can look vibrant and strong, or limp and dull, depending on your general condition and the way you treat it.

Here are some of the hints the top hairdressers have given our models to keep their hair in good shape. First, keep it clean. Shampoo at least once a week, oftener if necessary. Give your scalp a vigorous massage at least once a week, too. Brush your hair regularly with a natural-bristle brush. Have a conditioning treatment regularly, especially if your hair has been colored, bleached, permanented, or straightened.

Shampoo: First, brush briskly to loosen any scales on your scalp and to remove the old hair spray. Then massage your scalp. Using both hands, spread your stiff fingers over your head, pressing tightly against the scalp. Now make little circles with your hands so that your scalp moves with your fingers. Be sure to cover the entire area of the scalp and continue until it tingles.

Wet your hair thoroughly with warm water. Pour on shampoo and work up a good lather with your fingertips, using the same massaging motion. Rinse shampoo out completely with warm water, and shampoo again. Then rinse, rinse, and rinse again. End with a cold-water rinse if you can stand it. Towel-dry until most of the water is out. Wash out your comb and brush—there's no sense combing clean hair with a dirty comb.

Special Problems

OILY HAIR

Oily hair is a nuisance because it gets dirty too quickly. Shampoo it as often as necessary, using a special shampoo for this problem.

Don't use a shampoo that is too strong or full of alcohol in the hopes that it will dry out your hair—your sebaceous glands will only work overtime to compensate for it and you will be worse off. If you can't shampoo and your hair needs a cleaning, try a dry shampoo (if your hair isn't very dark) or a liquid dry cleaner. Or take a piece of cheesecloth, wrap it around your brush—and brush. The cheesecloth will pick up a lot of the oil and dirt. Another trick is to wipe strands of hair with cotton saturated with cologne. Keep your comb and brush scrupulously clean. Stay away from greasy and fatty foods, which make your glands produce more oil.

One method I've found works wonders for very oily hair is to steam it by putting hot towels around your head for ten minutes before you shampoo. Then, after shampooing with a detergent or egg shampoo, rinse with a little vinegar or lemon juice in warm water. Finally, massage some cologne directly into your scalp. Don't wear tight head coverings.

DRY HAIR

You, too, must steam your scalp. That's right. Steam it for ten minutes with hot towels wrapped around your head. Change the towel as often as necessary to keep it hot. Then, after parting your hair into half-

153

inch sections, rub olive oil into your scalp with pieces of cotton. Massage your scalp vigorously, allowing the oil to remain there for at least two hours. Then shampoo your hair with an oil-base shampoo, giving it only one soaping. Brushing is most important for you, too.

FINE HAIR

Fine hair usually doesn't keep a set very well, so have your hair carefully cut so that it will look good even when your set collapses. Don't try complicated hairdos. Get a body permanent or a regular one, perhaps, every six months. Try streaking or coloring to give the hair more body. When you shampoo, just give it one soaping and be sure to get all the soap out. Use a rinse that adds body to the hair. Towel dry, then apply a strong setting lotion. Try the gel variety or, perhaps, beer. Try them and see. Set your hair, using end papers or cotton. Never use brush curlers, and don't sleep on any rollers or your hair may begin to break. Before removing the rollers, spray with hair spray and allow to dry. Teasing is good for helping the set stay in, but do it only at the roots. After arranging your hairdo, spray, and don't brush out thoroughly for a couple of days. After that, give it a good brushing, teasing, and combing again.

TOO-CURLY HAIR

You can do one of two things if you want your hair to be straighter—you can straighten it or you can have it cut properly and work with it yourself. Straightening is best done by a professional, although there are some good home products on the market now. If you do it yourself, follow the instructions *exactly*. Your hair probably will not become completely straight. If you try to make it that way, you may overdo it and your hair can snap off. One expert recommends not straightening hair that's been bleached before coloring (which is the case when your hair's been turned a color that's lighter than your own shade) and he leaves the straightener on only the minimum time for tinted hair. Very thin, fine hair shouldn't be straightened at all. When your hair has been straightened, keep it covered in the sun, watch out for salt and chlorinated water. Oil treatments will restore some of the natural oil that is lost in straightening. Never have the straightening done oftener than every six months and always do it *before* coloring, at least one week before.

If you don't want a straightening job because it does complicate your life, be sure you get a good haircut. That is vital. Wear it short and work *with* the curl, or have it long and blunt cut. Set it on very large rollers with a strong setting lotion. Don't go out in the rain or the fog—your hair will always tend to curl in dampness. Try a curling iron pulled through the hair or an electric comb. That's what the models do at every sitting.

DANDRUFF

There are excellent dandruff-remover shampoos and preparations that can be obtained with a doctor's prescription. Ask his aid and advice, especially if your condition seems serious. Unchecked, dandruff can lead to serious skin problems. Try the steaming treatments before shampooing. Keep your brush and comb scrupulously clean.

Hair Coloring   155

It's a rare well-groomed and chic woman who doesn't color her hair today—I could count our natural-haired models on my fingers. Hair coloring is not exactly a new thought. Jezebel painted her eyebrows, Muhammad dyed his beard. Egyptian women went to great lengths to lighten their hair, while Roman women tried to bleach theirs with quicklime—often with rather sorry results. Today, with hair-coloring products in such an advanced and sophisticated stage, there's little worry that you'll end up like some of those shiny-domed Roman belles. The important thing is to have your tinting done by an expert professional colorist, or, if you do it yourself at home, to follow the instructions *to the letter*. The companies that perfected these products spent years and millions of dollars doing it, so don't improvise. It's possible to color your hair any shade at all, but should you? I maintain that a natural-looking color is essential and it should be one that compliments your skin tone. For example, bright red hair looks good on practically no one. And anyone with even a tinge of sallowness to the skin should never wear a color that has yellow in it. Olive-skinned girls will *not* have more fun as a blond or a redhead. Their skins will look dirty. The warm tones, such as chestnut, would be best. Test colors on yourself by trying on wigs, but never go really far from your own natural shade. Otherwise the maintenance might well be overwhelming—you need touch-ups much more frequently, and the further you go, the harder it is on your hair. Remember that hair should be abused as little as possible, and *anything* you do to it such as coloring, bleaching, straightening, permanenting makes it more fragile.

The ashy tones usually look best on most people, or perhaps the *slightly* reddened shades. But never go yellow blond, or raven black, or bright red. The big consideration really is your age. If you are over thirty, usually you'll look best with hair a bit lighter than your natural color—skin tones fade and darker color may be too harsh. Under that age, you are freer to experiment.

Once your hair turns gray, you really must color it a lighter tone than your original shade, if you color at all. A darker color will look artificial and unflattering. Often the best way to cope with mousy-gray hair is to highlight it. This means that you take strands of hair around the face and through the crown and have them bleached one or two or

three shades lighter than the base color. This gives a sun-kissed look. Be sure to avoid the stripy effect like the plague! You must be subtle.

I think the best way to choose a color is to go for a consultation to the best hair colorist in the nearest big city. Don't let unknown little operators work on you.

If you decide to do your own coloring (as I do), try a temporary rinse before you color it permanently. Before you do anything, follow the instructions about giving yourself a preliminary patch test to be sure you will not have an allergic reaction to the ingredients. This is necessary before each application as allergies are often inconsistent and may exist only at certain times. Also make a preliminary strand test to determine the color results on the hair. Home hair coloring is very much perfected now—I like the color I get myself better than at the salon, but I follow the rules to the letter!

Once your hair is colored, or bleached, remember that maintenance is a problem. It's a lot better to have your own mousy drab hair than a beautiful shade that has grown out and left mousy roots. You must be scrupulous about touch-ups—perhaps every month or six weeks. Your hair, having been made more dry and fragile by the coloring, will need regular conditioning treatments. Keep your hair covered in the sun, as its rays can fade or discolor it. If you get salt water or chlorinated pool water in your hair, give yourself a shampoo as soon as possible. Green or orange hair never did anyone any good.

157

Changing the color of your hair can make marvelous changes in your appearance. Just keep in mind that you've added one more problem to a perhaps already complicated life. It takes more care and grooming than a natural head of hair, so be sure you're the type who'll keep up with the upkeep.

Permanents

To tell the truth, I don't really like curling permanents because most hairdressers don't know how to give good ones. And a bad one is a misery. You end up with hair that wriggles rather than waves. But properly given, I do believe in body permanents. This is the kind that only adds body to your hair, makes it more manageable, holds a set longer. Rather than a curling permanent, I think it's better to put your own hair up—daily, if necessary.

Always get a rather light body permanent and be prepared to have another in a couple of months. If you're going to do the job at home, remember to follow directions to the letter. This is vitally important if it's to turn out right. Don't try to improve on the instructions or you may really be sorry (till all your hair grows out!). Be sure to give yourself a test curl before going ahead with the whole procedure, and be especially careful if you color, bleach, or straighten your hair. I've seen models' hair break to the roots for lack of care.

Never give yourself (or get) a permanent *and* a coloring or straightening job at the same time. Straightening or permanents should always be done *at least a week* before the coloring. Have your permanent before your next touch-up, if your hair is already colored.

Don't have a permanent if your hair isn't in good condition, you'll only make it more fragile. Give yourself a few conditioning treatments beforehand anyway.

I don't want to scare you away from permanents—I just want to caution you so you won't have trouble.

Hairpieces

Until recently, anyone who wore a wig or a hairpiece was bald or had very thin patchy hair to cover up. It was like wearing a fake leg—you did it because you had to. Today wigs and hairpieces are beauty tools and there are endless varieties available, at all prices and in almost every store. Full wigs, which can really transform you into a whole new person, have lost some of their initial popularity. They are expensive (or should be, if they are to look real), they tend to be hot, and they completely mash your own hair underneath. I still like them for the times when my hair is really a mess and I don't feel like doing anything about it, and I like the totally different effect. But, most of the time and for most women, I think hairpieces are much more useful.

One of the most effective pieces is the fall. This is a hank of hair that is placed about midway across your head, the hair falling to the back. It is usually held on to your head by an attached comb or a hair band. The fall can be long or short and can be worn a number of different ways— have your hairdresser demonstrate for you.

As for other hairpieces, there are separate little curls to be pinned on, long braids or pony tails, bangs, top thatches, and so forth. If you can

159

afford it, it's fun to have a whole wardrobe of them so that you can produce all kinds of effects. My models never go on a job without at least three or four, all of which they can maneuver into the most fetching arrangements.

This is the proper way to attach your hairpiece: crisscross two bobby pins or make a couple of pin curls in your own hair anchored by crisscrossed bobby pins. Then slide the little comb under these or attach with more bobby pins tucked away underneath. If you want to hide the line of demarcation between your hair and the piece, cover with a hair band, a bow, or just comb your own hair over the line, blending it well. Or you can make a ribbon of hair from the under section of the hairpiece and pull it across the line like a hair band, anchoring the end with a bobby pin.

Always buy the best hairpieces you can afford and be sure they match your own shade perfectly—otherwise you will *look* like you've slapped on a hank of someone else's hair. A hairpiece must look like it's your own in both color and texture. This is true for style, too. For example, it isn't attractive to wear a big chignon perched on top of a short cropped hairdo—obviously, it's a fake. Merge your own hair into the hairpiece so that the beautiful mop is all yours.

Take care of a hairpiece just as you do your own hair. Shampoo it when it gets dirty and set it on rollers. Use as little spray on it as possible.

Hairstyles

This is a very difficult thing to advise about unless I have you sitting right here with me—everyone has different features, figure needs, and desires. Even then, everyone can wear many styles, even the current "in" ones, if they are modified to suit her. First decide on the effect you want and what kind of life you lead. A career girl usually wants a style not too complicated but fairly chic. A housewife often desires something that is easy to care for at home and quite casual. A more socially inclined woman may want a more dressy hairdo, and usually has the time to go to the hairdresser frequently.

The haircut is the most vital step in a good hairdo and this is not a thing you can get anywhere. You must find the best haircutter you can, and explain to him just what it is you are after. And you must wear your hair in a way to which the cut lends itself. Without a good cut, you can have your hair set in the most interesting ways, only to have it collapse immediately.

The next thing is to consider the texture of your hair. Fine straight hair should be treated as though it will be cut only and never set. That way, when the set collapses, you won't be a wreck. If your hair is coarse, you can do pretty much anything with it. If it is too curly and you don't want to straighten it, don't choose a straight style as it will never work for you. Don't cut it too short, but leave it long enough to go over large rollers. If your hair is thin and fine, you'll need a fairly curly style. All of this your hairdresser will have to help you decide—so find a good one. It's worth traveling to the nearest large city every six weeks for a good haircut if your town doesn't have a good stylist.

Your face shape (as well as your build) should influence your hairstyle. If your face is long and narrow, don't wear it long and straight, but play down the shape by having your hair cut on a line with the mouth, and keep it flat on top with width on the sides. A round face can use length, perhaps with panels of hair coming onto the cheeks and a lift on top. Just as with makeup, you can produce optical illusions with hair.

161

A narrow forehead can look wider if the hair in this area extends out a bit. Small eyes will look larger by wearing bangs. Bangs also will minimize a low or a high forehead. A low forehead needs the bangs to start high on the head rather than at the hairline, while a high forehead requires bangs to start low.

A prominent nose can look smaller if you add some hair at the crown, and never have a center part.

If your neck is short, wear your hair quite short in back, though it can be longer at the sides. If your neck is long, you can conceal it with longer hair—but you don't have to. Long necks are fashionable right now.

Widen a narrow forehead by puffing out the hair at the temples; narrow a broad one by doing the opposite and curving the hair toward the face. Balance a heavy jaw by adding fullness toward the top of the head, or by curving the hair in front over your ears and onto your jaw.

The possibilities are endless, of course, so you'll have to experiment for yourself. My models have to keep their hair quite convertible so they wear it medium length, which looks good down or up and lends itself to the use of hairpieces. But then, they don't have important face-shape problems or they wouldn't be models.

In choosing a hairstyle, you must keep your age in mind. If you're not very young, it's best to stay away from very straight hairdos. Choose one that's a little wavy, a little fluffier, so that it will help soften any lines or wrinkles. Usually it's a good idea not to wear your hair long, and quite short is usually best. But don't get too curly around your face—that gives you a nervous look.

Setting Your Hair

All of our models must be really good at setting their own hair, because their hair must be perfect every single day and they can't spend their lives in the beauty salon. They learn, often from me, how to work with rollers and bobby pins, and they can do a professional job in five minutes. I'll try to explain to you how they do it.

162

Choose the right setting lotion for your type of hair. Some girls just use water, but I think most of us need something that will hold more strongly. Especially fine limp hair or very curly hair needs setting lotion, and often I find the gel type the best. And we've had good luck, as I've said, with sugar and water, or beer and water. (But remember beer is drying.) Experiment a bit to find the one that works best for you. If your hair is terribly fine and limp and doesn't hold a set well, completely dry it first before applying the setting lotion. And if you have a really serious problem, let the lotion dry, then reapply before setting.

You can apply the lotion to your entire head if you're a fast worker, or else wet down each strand at a time. Comb your hair in the directions you will set it in, then section it off as you go. Many girls find end papers very handy—fold a piece over the strand of hair you are about to roll or pin curl, slide it down to the ends, then roll. These are particularly good if your hair is not blunt cut, and therefore not all the same length.

Our girls all use rollers and for current styles they definitely are best. Of course, you will probably need pin curls for the very short hair in back or on the cheeks. To roll your hair, take a piece of hair about half an inch deep and no wider than the roller you'll be using. Apply the setting lotion and comb at an angle opposite to the direction you'll be rolling. Fold on the end paper, slipping it down to the end. Wind roller firmly from ends to roots; then clip the under side of the roller to your head so that it is firm but does not pull.

163

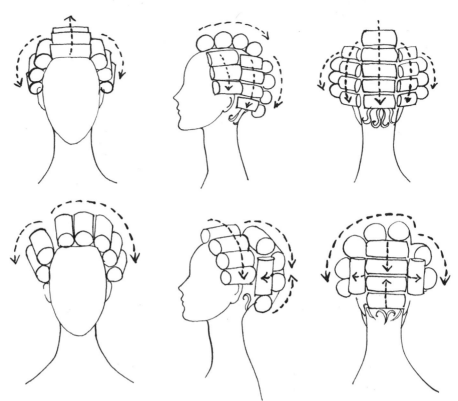

A word on rollers. You may use the hard-plastic kind or the mesh-covered wire ones. Never use the rollers with brushes inside. These do not leave a smooth curl, and they can be harmful to your hair as well as your scalp. Besides, they're uncomfortable. If you're going to sleep on them, you'll no doubt prefer the wire variety or perhaps the spongy ones (which aren't as good but better than not being able to sleep all night) .

The important thing in using rollers is to wind smoothly and tautly, taking up just the right amount of hair and clipping firmly. You must use the right size roller for the set you want—though most of our girls use the very large ones so that they get curves without curls. And you must set in some pattern. There are only a couple of really basic roller sets.

Pin curls are a little difficult to make perfectly. You have to make them round and smooth and all in the correct relationship and direction. But practice and you'll be an expert in no time. Hold a piece of your hair (no more than an inch around on your scalp) out from your head with one hand. Wind it around the index finger of the other for one turn. Slip it off and continue turning to the head. Clip flat to your head or just at the part closest to the scalp if you want it to stand out.

To set your bangs, you can use a wad of cotton just to give them a shape, and hold in place with a clip or some cellophane tape. Use tape, too, to keep short hair at the nape of the neck in place or to hold curls that turn onto the cheek.

The comb-out is the part that requires talent. Luckily, it's the kind of talent you can develop if you work at it. It's something that is hard to explain in words, so mostly you'll have to work, work, work before you'll have much success.

Be sure your hair is really dry before you take out the rollers and clips. If your hair does not keep a set well, spray with hairspray and let dry. Now brush your hair thoroughly—give it a real workout. Don't worry, it won't ruin your set if your hair is clean. If this is an in-between-shampoos setting and your hair is oily, then only brush a little. Now brush it into the shape you want, smoothing in the right directions with the brush. Flip up ends over your other hand, or flip under. You will probably need a little bit of teasing or back-brushing. Don't do much of this as it isn't good for your hair and puffy unnatural looking heads are no longer in fashion, I'm happy to say. Just tease a little right at the roots to give your hair some height where you need it. Then brush the top back into shape. Use a bit of hairspray if you need it. Not too much, for it tends to dull the hair, and make it get dirty faster. Spray *lightly,* holding the can at least a foot away from your head, and do it with sweeping motions.

17
Take Your Hands in Hand

After the face, the hands are the most expressive part of the body—if you look through any fashion magazine, or just watch people, you'll see how important hands are, too, in the total picture of a person. Hands should be as pretty and graceful as you can make them. This isn't difficult, but you've surely noticed how many attractive women take off their gloves to reveal hands that are chapped, or wrinkled, or have un-kempt nails, or chipped nail polish. And others who use their hands in an ungraceful, unattractive manner. Some shake hands like a rag gone limp. Some are always twisting a handkerchief, or clenching their fists, or moving their hands stiffly and self-consciously.

A model must know how to place her hands to the best advantage to be photographed, how to move them gracefully for a film. She must know how to keep them looking smooth and soft. You, too, will be able to use your hands more expressively and to keep them looking pretty if you take a little time to learn the tricks of hand care that I've taught our models.

First, let's go into the matter of skin care. The time when a doctor could tell a woman's age by her hands is gone. And so are "dishpan hands." *If* you make a little effort. If you've let your hands become anything less than lovely, I'm here to help you correct the situation. Today.

The skin of your hands has fewer oil cells than your face and the oil glands that supply the natural oil to the skin to keep it soft and supple have to work overtime to repair the damage wrought by the detergents and harsh cleaners we use today. This lack of oil makes for old and wrinkled hands if they are not protected.

When you work with your hands—gardening or doing housework—never let them go bare. Protect them by using a hand cream containing silicones, which form an invisible film over your skin. Gloves will give your hands added protection as well as preserve your manicure. Wear them for dishwashing or heavy cleaning or working out in the garden. Never go outdoors on a cold or windy day without wearing gloves.

Every time you wash your hands (of course, using a mild soap), dry them thoroughly, and cream them immediately. I've found that facial moisturizers make ideal hand creams if you need extra coverage.

Wear hand cream to bed every night. If your hands are beginning to mature, now is the time to enrich your skin with a moisturizer. If you've allowed your hands to get chapped, put on the cream and then a pair of cotton gloves for the night.

MANICURE

A weekly manicure must be fitted into your schedule, with touch-ups in between if necessary. Never let the total job go for longer than a week—your nails will have grown a bit during that time and no amount of touching up will look good.

Remove all old polish with an oily polish remover. Apply the remover with a piece of cotton, allowing it to soak in for a few seconds to soften the polish. Then wipe from the base of the nails outward until every trace of polish is gone.

Reshape the nails with an emery board. Do not file back and forth, but from one edge to the other, always in one direction. This helps prevent splitting. Now apply a cuticle oil or cuticle remover and push back the cuticles with an orange stick. Remove any hangnails with a

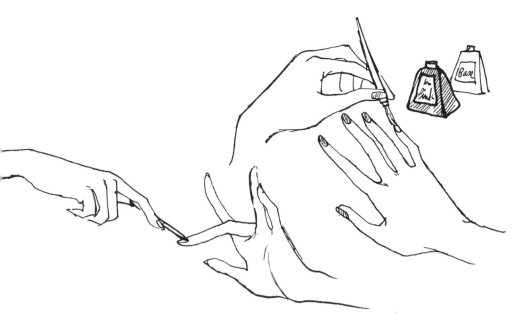

small scissors, but don't cut the cuticles. Cutting makes them grow back thicker and heavier and you'll always be working at them. Now buff your nails thoroughly. Clean under the nails with an orange stick wrapped in wet cotton.

Now you are ready for the polish—five coats of it. That's right, five coats! This will keep a good finish on your nails for at least a week. It won't take too long, maybe fifteen minutes.

Place one hand, fingers spread out, flat on a table. With the other hand, apply the polish. First, two base coats. Now two coats of color. Finally a sealing coat. Each coat must dry completely before you apply the next. Always brush from the base of the nail outward, using just enough polish to cover without any piling up. Cover the entire nail— white moons are passé. After you apply each coat, except for the sealer, remove just a hairline of polish from the edge of your nail by running your opposite thumb along it. This helps prevent chipping. Carry the sealer all the way to the edge and a bit under the nail as well.

Do your nails split easily? Try this trick. File your nails square across the tip. Allow them to grow this way. Apply a coat of sealer, over your polish, on your nails nightly, both on top and underneath. Keep doing this until you give yourself the next manicure. It strengthens your nails wonderfully. Do not shape the nails until they are long enough to

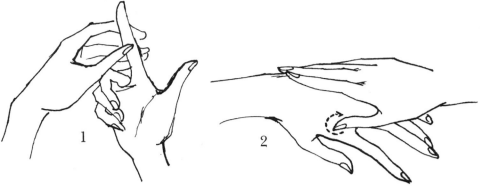

maintain a nice solid base at the bottom and never file them downward at the sides.

Some people have great luck with the new nail hardeners. Follow the directions on the bottle.

If you have long nails and one of them cracks, make a patch of an old linen hanky or buy a package of patches. Remove all polish and apply the patch with a nail fix, which you can buy at the drugstore. Now reapply the polish. If a nail breaks off, file the edge smooth. If you like, you can apply a fake nail cut to the right shape until your own nail grows or maybe a patch of powdered nail lengthener. Never wear your nails longer than a half inch beyond the end of your fingers—long spiky nails are not pretty and they break easily. If you type or play the piano or do much housework, you'll be best off growing them only about an eighth of an inch beyond your fingertips.

Don't let your nail polish clash with either your lipstick. or your clothes. Choose a color that blends with most of your wardrobe, or stick to a pale pink shade that you can wear with everything except the orange tones. If you decide to wear orange, change the polish, too.

EXERCISES FOR THE HAND

Hands, to be graceful, must be relaxed, serene, and poised, with attractive movements. I have several hand exercises that our models find helpful. If you practice them faithfully, you should see great improvement in the control you have over your hands. You must also consciously avoid fussing with your jewelry or your hair, twisting your hands together, picking at the lint on your clothes, clenching your hands, chewing on your fingers, or any of those other not very attractive motions you might find yourself doing.

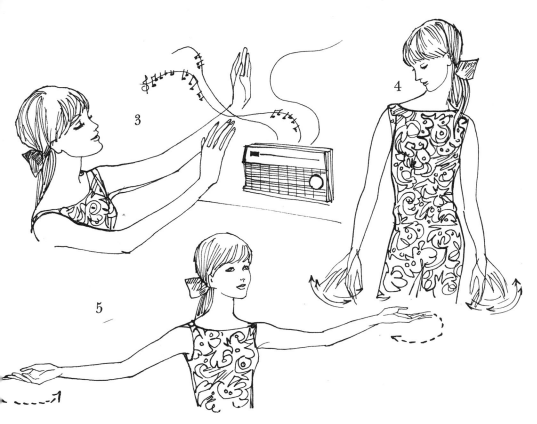

1. Cream your hands, then massage each finger individually with thumb and forefinger of the other hand. Gently pull each finger from the top to the nail tip. Then stroke the cream from the knuckles to the wrist, using the same action you would use fitting a new pair of gloves.

2. Use the fingers of one hand to massage the skin on the back of the other hand, and with your thumb, gently rotate the skin on the knuckles at the base of the fingers.

3. Turn on the radio to a symphonic program and pretend you are conducting the music with a gentle wrist movement and an open palm.

4. Drop your hands to your sides, letting them hang there like dead weights. Then open them, spreading the fingers wide apart. Hold while you count ten. Relax and shake vigorously from the wrists without any arm motion. This not only strengthens the muscles in the back of the hands, but it is relaxing and you can do it almost anywhere.

5. Lift both hands with palms up to shoulder height, elbows slightly relaxed. Slowly bring hands, not elbows, forward with palms facing up. Now turn palms down and drop hands slowly.

171

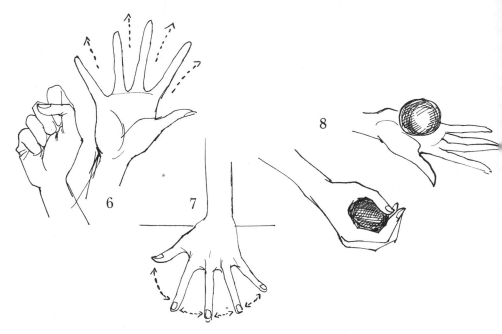

6. Make a fist and hold it tight for a count of five. Fling hand open with fingers separated.

7. Place your hands on a table. Stretch your fingers as far apart as possible and hold for a count of twenty. Relax. Repeat five times.

8. Open and close your fingers over a rubber ball (the harder the better), pushing deep into the ball.

After exercising the hands, dip them into warm water and immediately massage a moisturizer into the skin—when you are warm, the cream is better absorbed.

Practice different ways to hold your hands—hanging in a relaxed fashion at your sides when you stand, resting serenely in your lap or on the arm of the chair (*resting* on the arm, not *holding* it). Almost anything looks good, so long as it is *relaxed,* rather than stiff or self-conscious. Study some of my models in the magazines, and you'll get some good ideas for your hands. G., one of our most successful models last year, found her hands her biggest problem—she just didn't know what to do with them. With these relaxing exercises and a conscious effort to calm down, along with some help from photographers and fellow models, her hands have become one of her assets and you see them in every magazine. Your hands may never be famous, but they *can* be pretty.

173

18
Varieties of the Bath

A girl can be pretty as a picture and as charming as can be, but if she isn't well-groomed, all is lost. Good grooming means that she is clean and sweet-smelling, neat and carefully tended—all over. It means that she bathes every day, makes sure her hair is in good shape, her nails clean and manicured, her legs free of hair, her eyebrows tweezed, her buttons all on, her hems neat, her underclothes clean and sewn, her shoes shined—all those little things that add up to someone who's nice to be near.

If you've been reading carefully, you already know how to tend your nails, your feet, your legs, your hair. You have to be sure to apply the advice as often as necessary. Go over your clothes as you take them off to be sure they need no repairs or cleaning. Wash your underthings every day. Polish your shoes (and your handbags) before you put them away for the night. Get rid of unwanted hair. Under your arms, use a razor or a depilatory and then an effective deodorant or antiperspirant—every single day.

Now everyone thinks she knows how to take a bath. But a bath can be anything you wish to make it. You can take a quick, no-time-wasted bath or a shower that stimulates and invigorates. You can take a relaxing bath. Or a luxury beauty bath. Or a therapeutic bath.

1. The quickie. A shower is best for this. If you take a fast shower when you get up in the morning, it will leave your skin tingling and refreshed. Keep the water hot for several minutes; then gradually cool it off. Soap up and rinse off. Jump out and dry yourself vigorously with a terry towel. Splash on your favorite cologne. This kind of "wetting" will clean you, all right, but you won't derive the same benefits you would from a lazy tub bath. "I know, I know," you're going to say, but you don't have the time in the morning, what with the demands of a time clock to meet, or a husband rushing off to work, or the baby to tend to. . . . So, plan to take time at night for that tub ceremony.

175

2. The relaxing bath. A bath for just pure relaxation is a real necessity in this jet age. It will smooth those old nerves and ready you for a good night's sleep. Gather together all your bath props: bath oil or crystals, a rich fragrant soap, dusting powder, cologne—all matching in scent; and a foam-rubber headrest. Pour a few drops of oil in the tub under the faucet, turn on the hot water alone for a few seconds to release the full fragrance of the oil, then continue filling with warm water. Slowly sink down into the water, lie back on your pillow, and close your eyes. Try to forget all the problems of the day. After twenty minutes or so of this, you should feel like a real lazybones. But now is the time to go to work. Lather your sponge or washcloth to a rich suds and give yourself a going over. Be sure to reach all those out-of-the-way places, using a long-handled brush if necessary. Now up and out. Pat yourself dry; give yourself a dusting of bath powder and a spray of cologne from top to toe. Now to bed and pleasant dreams.

3. The beauty bath. This is nothing new—it's been a ritual for centuries. Poppaea, beautiful wife of Emperor Nero of Rome, took baths

in asses' milk. Mary, Queen of Scots, preferred to bathe in fragrant wine. Skip the milk and the wine—and try our way.

You'll need: a bath tray that attaches to the side of the tub to hold beauty mask, face cream, throat cream, a mirror, eyebrow tweezers, pumice stone, hand mitt, and soap.

Cleanse face before getting into the tub. Pour in bath oil or crystals. If your skin is dry, add a glass of plain old starch to the water and swish it around until it dissolves. Hop in. Apply the mask to your face. While waiting for it to harden, look at your eyebrows. Are there any straggly hairs? Take care of them. When the mask is nearly dry, rinse it off. Pat face dry with washcloth. Now smooth the face cream over your face, patting gently around the eyes and stroking gently upward from the base of the neck to the chin. These little occupations give enough time for the softening of the skin around the backs of your heels and elbows, so scrub off the dead scales with a pumice stone. How about your fingernails? Gently push back the cuticle, making things twice as easy for your manicure later on.

177

Now, time to relax. Stretch out and soak for a good half hour—I like to set a timer to remind me when the thirty minutes are up. Then reach for your hand mitt, lather it with soap, and start scrubbing. When you're spanking clean, stand up, turn on the shower, and let a spray of cool, then cold, water splash over you. Or turn on the tub faucet and splash. Out of the tub, wrap yourself in a big terry towel and pat yourself dry. When the skin is still slightly moist, spray on cologne and skin lotion. *Voilà!*

4. Finally, there is the therapeutic bath. To really stir up your circulation so that your blood seems to be racing through your body, I suggest that you invest in a water circulator, either the installed kind or the less expensive gadget that attaches to the faucet. Before getting in, scatter a half cup of mineral bath crystals in the tub, and keep the water temperature around 100 degrees. Relax while the water swirls around you.

In this day when so much emphasis is put on products to make us smell sweet as clover, you must be aware of the fact that taking a bath every day will not guarantee to keep you fresh all the time without some outside help in the form of a deodorant or antiperspirant. A bath will temporarily banish unpleasant odors, but bacteria can develop again on the skin, even shortly after you've bathed. The sweat glands, especially those under the arms, set up their normal action, and, in a little while, that unwanted odor starts up again.

A deodorant checks the odor and helps prevent perspiration. The antiperspirant actually checks the perspiration flow. There are many varieties of each: liquid, cream, roll-ons, powder, soap. And don't let the idea of checking perspiration bother you—it won't hurt you to stop the action from a few sweat glands—you've got millions of others all over your body.

Some women rarely need to use an antiperspirant; others need it daily. I find it's best to use it at night, letting it set before you do anything strenuous that will make you perspire.

There are also deodorant powders and soaps that you might try if you think you need them.

Always spray on cologne or use a bit of perfume—but take it easy. Don't asphyxiate the people around you!

179

19
A Word to the Mother of a Teen-ager

It is never too early to start on the road to beauty. From the day you first teach a child to wash her face and brush her teeth, you have started her on her own beauty program.

I taught my daughters to brush their hair twice daily from the moment they were old enough to hold a brush. Today at nineteen, my oldest daughter, Jamie, can devise the most elaborate coiffures and I have to put only the finishing touches on the golden locks of eight-year-old Lacey and ten-year-old Katie.

If you will instill in your own children the importance of taking care of their skin by keeping it clean, and their hair by brushing it, and their clothes by hanging them up and, of course, making certain that their shoes are always well polished, you will be starting them on good grooming habits that will carry them through life. Even if you have to say it till you're hoarse, make sure that your teen-age daughter gives her complexion the care it needs, so that when she reaches young womanhood and throughout her life as she matures, her skin will glow. She may fight you for a few short years, but she will spend the rest of her days thanking you.

Make sure that she learns about diet and exercise. Make sure that she knows what to eat and why. You can't expect her to bypass French fries and chocolates in favor of an apple if she doesn't know the reason.

A teen-age girl may seem reluctant to accept your advice, because, after all, she feels herself capable of solving the problems of the world. However, she is beginning to be interested in boys and the best way to attract them is through looking her best.

As teen-agers tend to exaggerate, I sincerely believe that it is much better for you to introduce her to makeup yourself, rather than let her pile it on herself.

You can learn from this help as well as she can and perhaps you will find that learning to be beautiful together will bring you closer than you have been in some time.

If your child has problem skin, get her on my pamper plan for oily or disturbed skin and make her stick to it. Watch every single thing that she puts into her mouth, remembering what I have said about nutrition. Eggs, chocolate, nuts, candy, fried foods, gravy, bacon, cold cuts, mayonnaise, strawberries, soft drinks, ice cream, cream, and cakes can all contribute to the downfall of your child's good complexion.

181

At a time like this, three-times-a-day cleansing will not hurt. Stay away from medicated lotions, medicated makeups, and beauty grains, unless the doctor recommends them. These will not solve the problem, and may further complicate her woes. Even if it means changing your family's eating habits for a while, change them. Give your child the gift of good skin. May I say that this is good for teen-age boys, too.

Make sure that her hair is clean. Avoid bangs if she has a problem skin, as the oil from the hair will only further irritate the skin. If she needs a dandruff-remover shampoo, make certain that there is always one handy. Help her to set her hair and be enthusiastic. Get her a subscription to some fashion and beauty magazines geared to young people. Turn her interest toward the things that make a woman lovelier.

Posture is as important to your daughter as it is to you. Do posture exercises with her. Study her problems with her and help her to grow up beautifully. It may be that she can teach you a few tricks herself. There is nothing like a teen-age daughter prodding her mother to keep interested and young.

If you set a time for weekly conferences, do, and don't allow anything to make you break it. Youngsters learn by watching and your daughters are watching you.

They look to you for guidance on the thorny path of growing up. It is part of a girl's instinct to want to grow up to dress in fashion and to use makeup. If our girls are going to learn to face life, we should teach them to do it with their best face forward. If you teach your youngster sound and wholesome ways of looking her best, you have given her a gift that she will never lose during her lifetime.

20
The Maturing Beauty

Are you frankly "over forty" and enjoying every minute of it?
Or have you retired into that unattractive haven known as middle age?
If you have kept up your appearance and your interests are varied, the
chances are the world is your oyster and you are making the most of it.
There's no excuse for you, whatever age you are, to sit and watch life

go by. Actually, this is just the moment when you should be ready to take a *new* lease on life—the children have flown, family responsibilities are diminished, and you have many years left to charm and conquer, so make the most of them. Maturity is a wonderful time if you allow it to be—and you can continue to be just as attractive as you ever were.

Now, I don't mean that you must try to look like your twenty-year-old daughter. There is nothing more UNattractive than an older woman seeking to retain her lost youthful bloom by wearing way-out makeup, junior clothes, or a coiffure that looks fine on a teen-ager, but not on her. Trying to regain youth in this manner is a great mistake. And why should you want to? Face the facts—and the calendar. Then do your darnedest to look just as beautiful as you possibly can. It's possible for every one of us to look years younger than our age.

Just because you are over forty, your skin does not have to show it. Women, as they grow older, are often lax in the care they give the skin—they just plain give up the good fight. There is no reason at all why anyone, any age, should lose out on the glamour sweepstakes. Some women lose their most interesting qualities through ignorance, while others just don't care. If you belong to the former group, you with my help can do something to remedy this, and if you are in the latter, it is time you took heed. There are too many lovely brunets and ravishing blonds just lying in wait for any attractive husband who may be losing interest in a dowdy wife.

As we grow older, care of the skin becomes increasingly important. The moist look that goes with youth is due to the natural oils and moisture. As we mature, we lose this precious oil and moisture, and it must be replaced. An aging skin shows lines and wrinkles that will become more pronounced if not attended to daily. And by wrinkles, I don't mean the smile lines (which are now easy to get rid of anyway—see my chapter on plastic surgery, etc.) or those interesting crevices that spell c-h-a-r-a-c-t-e-r, but just those lack-of-care lines.

184

An older skin becomes "crepey" in spots and sometimes discolored, especially at the neckline. Look at your throat—does it lack firmness? Has the skin tone changed over the years? What is needed is a moisturizer and possibly some peanut oil to penetrate deep into the tough skin of the neck. Start from the collarbone and gently massage up to the jawbone outward to the tip of the ears.

Smooth out the squint lines outside your eyes with peanut oil, too. And get in the habit of wearing sunglasses in the brilliant sun to prevent some of them developing in the first place.

Every woman, no matter what her age, must start *now* to take proper care of her skin. You can be sure that our models are taking care of theirs, and as long as I have anything to say about it, *daily* skin care will be on their agenda. And this is what YOU should have been doing all these years. However, a lot can be done to remedy neglect, if you will determine to buckle down and follow my beauty course.

An older skin needs stimulation as well as oil and moisture. A *light* astringent should be patted on daily. A mask treatment is a once-a-week must. For the dry skin, use the cream or jelly type; for the oily skin, you may prefer the kind that hardens and feels just like a mask. Be sure to read the directions and follow them closely. Actually, those of us who were plagued with a very oily skin in youth are the lucky ones now. While we hated that "shine" then, an oily complexion will maintain its natural elasticity longer.

As you get older, remember that good posture is vital. When you glanced into your mirror recently, were you startled to see that hump at the back of your neck? Did you notice a sagging chin line? Were your shoulders rounded, making you appear years older than your last birthday? This all comes from poor posture. Straighten up for a transformation. Go back over my chapter on posture where you will find exercises for your individual problem, jot them down, and practice these EVERY DAY with no fudging. It will take time to correct these posture flaws, and doing the exercise on a now-and-then basis will do exactly no good at all. Watch your stance when you walk, and watch the way you sit. Many older women manage to get themselves into sitting positions that even their teen-age daughters would not be guilty of. To ward off the appearance of age, you must remain supple and limber. And this means exercise—daily. Turn back to my exercise chapter. Do the general exercises plus any for your particular figure needs.

Your weight should be watched carefully, and this means a regular

185

diet to be adhered to ALWAYS. Figure out the necessary daily calorie count to keep you healthy, and stick to it. You do not need as many calories now as you did in your body-building days, but you do need high-protein foods. This weight-watching is especially important during the menopause—somehow insidious little particles of fat make their way into unwanted places and attach themselves there just like homing pigeons; to stay, if nothing is done about it. It's just as easy to eat the right foods as the wrong ones. If you will look at my diets and the list of foods I have given, you will find that you can eat nicely and heartily, and have fun doing it too!

Now for your hair. Is it in that intermediate stage or is it a soft gray? Make up your mind whether gray hair is to be your friend or foe. If your friend, dramatize it with striking colors in your clothes. Some find that, with the advent of white hair, they can now wear colors that used to be unbecoming to them, such as bright purples, gay reds, brilliant blues. This again depends upon your complexion. Be adventurous, try different shades and by the trial-and-error method decide which are your best colors. If you find that the pale pastels bring out a Dresden charm, then by all means keep to these muted tones. I think that gray hair is usually at its best when contrasted with a bright color—it gives a lift and adds zest and this is what is needed at this time of life.

The question of whether to tint or not to tint may be in your mind. This all depends on you, as the song goes. You may like gray hair; does your husband? A man may prefer that the girl of his youthful dreams continue to try to look the same as she did when he married her (a big mistake, which sometimes accounts for a woman who should have a mature charm still looking like a Kewpie doll). He figures that while she may not be able to keep her body perennially young, by golly, she sure can keep her hair the same color! There is just one hitch to this thinking. As we grow older, everything about us undergoes a subtle change. The skin tone changes gradually and sometimes the shade of our crowning glory of girlhood is definitely out of key with our new complexion. For instance, jet-black hair on a young girl with clear skin is ravishing. But try that jet-dye job on a gray-haired woman and it will probably do nothing except accentuate her age and make her look hard, no matter how expertly it has been applied. Keep the colors soft.

If you really prefer your hair the distinctive gray intended by nature, then keep it that way—a silvery halo that softens your skin tones and is characteristic of YOU. A blue or silver rinse will take away the yellow and bring out the gray highlights. Be sure it is a light rinse, none of these lavender, purple, or blue atrocities. Sometimes a steel gray is becoming, but this shade may bring out the yellow in a sallow skin, so watch out! If you are in that salt-and-pepper stage, I believe in tinting to match your former natural shade until the gray comes forth in all its cloudy glory.

If you want to change the color of your hair, always make it just a bit lighter than your original natural color. Stay away from yellow tones, aim more for the ashy or beige shades. And remember that red (and black, as I've mentioned) have a tendency to make mature women look hard.

My final advice about your hair is that it must always be well taken care of. A weekly trip to the hairdresser is absolutely necessary—unless of course you are one of those superior persons who can handle a rinse and "dress" your hair yourself. A soft wave is best—those tight ringlets are OUT for you. Some older women want a "tight" wave because it lasts longer, but what good is that if it shortchanges you on your looks? And straight hair, on the other hand, is usually not good either for mature women. The softness of a wave helps soften lines and droops.

Keep an eye on your makeup. The harsh, bright colors of the forties are taboo. And so are the very light lipstick tones that tend to make you look pasty and washed out. Best colors for you are the pastels—pinks and corals. Powder your lips before applying your lipstick to prevent any running lines. Match your base and powder to your skin if your skin is average. If your complexion is sallow, a foundation with a pink tone helps to remove the yellow. Or try one of those new moisturizer creams with a violet hue—it will warm up your skin. If you have a ruddy complexion, beige base and foundation are best. A pale complexion can be helped by blushers that have a pink element.

187

If your eyebrows have lost some of their color, brush a pale-gray pencil over them to give a frame to your eyes. Never use a dark-color pencil or you will look like a revival of the Vampire. As you see, your entire makeup should be keyed to pale tones. This is true, too, of eye shadow—but, of course, do use it. Perhaps a pale lavender, a light blue, or gray-green for evening, or beige or gray for daytime, but apply sparingly, please.

The one exception to the "light touch" is mascara. I think black mascara is best on everyone. If that's too much for you, use dark brown— but never lighter. Apply lightly, being sure never to end up with blobs on the lashes.

Your hands should always be kept well manicured. Because there are few oil ducts in this area, the skin here dries out more quickly than elsewhere. A hand cream full of beneficial moisturizers should be used at night and in the morning. Carry small packets of hand cream in your purse so that during the day after each washing you can pat it into your hands to soften the effects of the daily rinsings. Hand exercises are now more important than ever, to keep your hands flexible. See my chapter on hand care for these. If you are troubled with brown spots, they can be made less noticeable with the use of a cream bleach or they can be covered with a preparation made especially for the purpose of covering blemishes. This is also good for helping to make large veins less conspicuous. When applying your hand cream, start at the fingertips and smooth down over the wrists, massaging each finger on the way down. Pat some of the cream into your elbows—they become very "crepey" if no attention is paid to them.

Nothing can make you look older or more tired than feet that hurt. Aching feet can put a frown on your face quicker than anything. So make a weekly pedicure a habit. Smooth out the rough skin at the heels, rub in a refreshing moisturizer, oil around the base of the nails, and give them a coat of polish. Polish on both hands and feet (to match, naturally) should be in a light tone, just as the rest of your makeup is in a light key. Pale polish on nails gives a finish to your hands but does not attract attention to them as a bright lacquer would.

The selection of your wardrobe is most important. Now you must look for "line" and perfect fit. You will have to spend more time and more money on your clothes—those "little" dresses that you loved to buy are no longer for you. You need the more expensive things that are better tailored and better cut and have a style not to be found too easily in inexpensive clothes. All right, you say you can't afford to pay more? Well, this is what you do—buy *one good dress* instead of three cheap ones. You may not have so many different things to wear, but you will be assured of looking and feeling superb each time you step out. Elegance in your dress is called for now. Stay away from both the cute little styles and the matronly ones, and look for quiet simple lines with interesting fabrics and colors. Also be sure that hemlines are even and the correct length and that there is no middle sag at the waistline. These things give a matronly appearance. Last word of advice—now that you have beautiful clothes, show them off well with a beautiful posture.

At this writing, there's the possibility of a great new development for older women. According to some reputable doctors, the whole process of aging can be slowed down by replacement of a hormone, estrogen, which diminishes in the body as a woman approaches menopause. After menopause, natural production of estrogen eventually disappears altogether. Replacement of the hormone, the doctors say, can not only prevent discomforts of menopause but also can ward off wrinkled and sagging skin, brittle bones, dowager's hump, joint pains, heart disease, skin discoloration, and other symptoms of an aging body.

A qualified physician must determine the need for and the amount of estrogen replacement of each woman—this is nothing you can decide for yourself. So far, no harmful side effects have been noted, but research is still going on.

Of course, estrogen replacement is not the fountain of youth—the body ages in many ways unrelated to menopause and its effects. But it may well keep a woman more youthful, feminine, and attractive many years longer than she would have been without it. I'm going to try it—I'll let you know the results.

Perhaps of primary importance when you get older is your ATTITUDE. Are you resisting the change that is occurring in your life? Or are you facing up to it, realizing that this can be a wonderful period with

189

many new things to do and new horizons to investigate? Age, after all, is really a matter of spirit and, to keep the spirit young, you must be active, and I mean mentally as well as physically. Join groups of interest to you. Do you like art? Take up painting—you don't have to be a Leonardo da Vinci to get pleasure out of slapping paint on a canvas. Have you always wanted to write? Take a writing course at one of the adult education schools—you may be surprised at what you can turn out! Or be a hospital volunteer—understaffed as hospitals are, they will welcome you with open arms. The world needs your help.

So go to it. You may be your age, but you surely don't need to look it, or even more important, feel it.

21
Special Problems–
for Specialists

It's impossible to give a precise definition of beauty. It is different things to different people. In a woman, it is an impression of harmony in pleasant features along with a happy attitude, the effect heightened by makeup and grooming. Most of us can achieve at least a kind of beauty if we know how to make the most of what features we've got.

All of our models—as well as just about all of the secretaries, teachers, homemakers, schoolgirls, and so on who have sought our help for personal reasons—have developed a beauty all their own.

Occasionally, however, a woman has one feature, one physical characteristic, which needs expert outside help so that it may harmonize with the rest of her appearance. It may be a real block to beauty for her. It is only in such an instance that I suggest physical correction, either to future models or to women who simply desire fulfillment of their beauty potential.

We sometimes advocate cosmetic surgery or dental correction or, more frequently, electrolysis to remove excess hair—but we suggest these things only after considering the problem carefully. They should not be undertaken lightly, never to satisfy a whim or a wish to "just look different." They are only for those who have real handicaps, which cannot otherwise be overcome. In such cases, I heartily recommend correction by a specialist. Luckily, it is no longer considered a vain and foolish act to have a grotesque nose remodeled or to have a fanglike tooth filed or capped. If such features have been obstacles in the search for a happy, healthy outlook on life, the decision to remodel may be a very wise one.

Once you have decided to go ahead with the project, you must find a plastic surgeon, a dentist or orthodontist, an electrologist, or whatever, with a flawless reputation. No other will do. And you must be prepared to find out that perhaps he does not think you need the operation you are after. No ethical doctor will change a nose he thinks he cannot improve. No reputable dentist will put caps on attractive, healthy teeth. Rather, they will tell you that a shocking portion of their consultation time is spent convincing women that they do *not* need that new nose, that chin, the front teeth. This is serious business, and they have enough handicaps to work on. Remember, too, that there might well be a consultation fee. "Shopping" can be expensive!

192

NOSE SURGERY

This is one of the most basic and by far the most frequent of the plastic operations. The average "problem" nose is the large one, professionally termed the "Mediterranean nose." It has a pronounced curve, sometimes a real hook. At one time and by some standards, such noses were considered handsome, but American standards of beauty are such that too much nose, however classic in shape, can be a real flaw in otherwise harmonious features.

Two of our most exciting models, D. and N., had already begun work as Ford models when they decided to have nose surgery. Each was motivated by the realization that her nose was keeping her from becoming one of our top models. Certain poses, certain photographers, were not for them. Following their surgery, each girl was booked for twice the number of sittings she had had previously. And, because they felt more confident of their beauty, their nonprofessional lives became more rewarding too.

Large noses can be corrected by a comparatively simple operation that is basically the removal of cartilage. "Dished in" or "saddle noses" can be built up with skin and cartilage grafting. Too-wide noses and noses with bulbous tips are more difficult to rectify. Often they may be helped; sometimes they cannot.

Your doctor will give you an idea of the nose shape you will have after surgery. He will never agree to create, say, a nose identical to that of your favorite movie star—he must work with what you've got to start with.

Don't have a nose operation—or any plastic surgery—unless you've got a few weeks during which to hide. You'll be quite swollen and black and blue for a while. As for pain, different people have different thresholds. Nose surgery does indeed involve pain, despite the many modern palliatives that have brought it to a minimum. However, the very fact that thousands of people undergo nose surgery every month, without drastic interruption of their daily lives, is indication that the pain is far from unbearable.

SETTING BACK EARS

We frequently suggest this operation to our models. Protruding ears can be held back with spirit gum during a photographic sitting, but heat does drastic things to the gum's adhesive qualities. The "setting back" operation is such a quick and relatively simple procedure and it can forever end the risk of a sudden "pop!" of the released ears during costly photography. It is relatively painless.

SKIN PLANING/OR ABRASION

Done by a skilled plastic surgeon by sanding or wire-brush treatment, this procedure can minimize bumps and pits and finely wrinkled skin as well as various birthmarks such as "port wine" stains (tattooing— insertion of flesh-colored pigment—is sometimes used on these, too). Usually it is used to smooth out acne pits. It may not give one hundred per cent correction but it can make the complexion more adaptable to beauty treatment and cosmetics.

While I'm on the subject of acne pits, let me say that they should never be there in the first place. Acne is not a normal phase of adolescence. The moment any sign of acne appears, a young person should be taken to a good dermatologist. Immediately. There is no need to go through life with unsightly scars.

I recently nipped in the bud an "It will go away" case of acne. None too soon; the condition was almost in full bloom. When this girl first came to see us, I thought, "She has real possibilities. But she's got the measles!" She repeated the familiar refrain: "Oh, it's just adolescent skin. Mother says it's normal for someone my age. It will go away." Mother definitely did not know best in this instance. The dermatologist to whom we immediately sent her *did* know. Not only did a nice, healthy skin emerge because of his treatments but scars that would have blighted her life were prevented. Result: a most promising modeling career was launched.

FACE LIFTING

Our agency receives a lot of mail from maturing women, asking about face lifting. This is an intricate method of redraping the facial skin by cutting away any excess. The lift may last from five to ten years, and then must be done again. Don't consider it until your face really begins to show its age, and even then, long and thoughtful exploration of every

194

other means, every other road to beauty, should precede consultation on this step. If you decide to go ahead, pick no one but the *most* competent plastic surgeon, and don't expect miracles. You will undoubtedly look years younger, but you will never look like a twenty-year-old again. There will always be some scarring—after all, plastic surgery involves cutting, but usually the scars are very fine and can be hidden by your hair or by makeup.

Sometimes fairly young women develop "bags" over or under the eyes and these can be remedied by plastic surgery. The small scars can be concealed by makeup until they are completely healed, but you'll have to wear dark glasses for a couple of weeks.

BREAST SURGERY

Pendulous breasts are a true physical handicap to some women. Plastic surgery can reshape and reduce them, though it is an intricate and costly procedure. Again search out the best doctor. I do not recommend any of the new operations for building up the breasts. Wear falsies and wait until the methods have been perfected.

SILICONE FACE LIFTING

This is a new method of injecting silicone subcutaneously to fill out indented hollows and wrinkles. It promises to be a marvelous thing, but at this writing, it has not yet been approved by the Food and Drug Administration, and is only experimental. What it does is plump up the indentations, raising them to the level of the rest of the skin. It will be used mainly for frown lines, forehead wrinkles, deep mouth lines. I know several people, including myself, who have tried it with great results.

ELECTROLYSIS

Because of the temptation to let the flattering light at a dressing table shadow the truth, many women seem unaware of the handicap of excess facial hair. But we find we recommend this kind of correction with surprising regularity to our potential models. Electrolysis is the one good approved method for eradicating this excess hair. It can banish a "mous-

195

tache," oust unsightly chin hairs, and do away with overabundant side-burns. It can also heighten the hairline that may grow much too low. I recommend no dillydallying if you need this treatment. Keep in mind that makeup will not hide a lot of hair or fuzz—remove it!

TOOTH CORRECTION

Problem teeth, which mar the looks of an otherwise good mouth and pretty smile, can be helped in several ways by a dental specialist. Your teeth can be capped, or evened, or straightened.

Of course, early adolescence is the very best time for teeth-straightening, but an adult need not accept crooked, unaligned teeth either. The orthodontist will tell you to what extent your teeth can be corrected. The process will involve perhaps unattractive braces for a couple of years, but it will be well worth it—and heaven knows you won't be alone. Practically no one goes around with badly crooked teeth anymore. It costs money, however, so you'll have to scrimp a bit.

Tooth capping is not for everyone who dreams of a dazzling new smile, but it can make a whole new you. An ethical dentist may agree to jacket perfectly healthy teeth only if he feels the work is absolutely warranted. If your teeth are yellow or poorly shaped, find out what the possibilities are for you.

The evening of teeth can be a very simple matter. One of our most promising applicants eliminated her tooth problem in one short inexpensive sitting. One of her incisors was noticeably longer than the others, and it interfered with her bite. A session with a dentist made all the difference between a self-conscious grotesque smile and a beautiful one.

CHOOSING THE SPECIALIST

It's always a problem finding the proper specialist. Since everyone has her own dentist, help for dental disfigurements can be found most readily. Ask your dentist to recommend the right man for you.

There are good electrolysis specialists in nearly every community, but remember two things. First, shop for the very best one through your doctor or the local medical society, and by careful inquiry. Second, once you have found what you believe to be the right one, insist on a trial treatment on some portion of your skin that is relatively unnoticeable. (If the specialist is good, this test will be automatic anyway.) Only a test can determine if your skin can take the treatment without scarring. Almost everyone can be successfully treated.

In seeking a good plastic surgeon, be meticulous. It is vital to avoid a charlatan and, in any profession, there are those. Ask your doctor to recommend the best surgeon he knows, or check with your county medical society to which many reputable doctors belong. This is not absolute proof that a doctor is perfect, nor is the fact that a doctor does not belong a sign that he is not a good, ethical, capable man. However, the society is an excellent aid to those who have no other means of choosing a plastic surgeon. Once you've found out who among its members is qualified, take your next precaution: find out if the suggested doctor is a member of the American Board of Plastic Surgeons, the American Society of Plastic and Reconstructive Surgery, the American Association of Plastic Surgery. He can belong to all, or, again, to none and still be competent. But membership can be a guide when you have no other means of making sure.

Once you've chosen your man, visit him for a consultation. He'll tell you if and how much he can help you. Then go home and think it over. If your Cyrano nose is really interfering with your life, probably plastic surgery is right for you. Or perhaps a markedly receding chin ruins your appearance, or your face is a mass of wrinkles—the decision is up to you (and the surgeon) whether or not you should go through with the operation.

The cost varies from city to city, from physician to physician, from case to case. Only your doctor can quote you an exact price—but everything costs money in our world, and especially plastic surgery.

22
All in All

Now the preaching is over, you've heard all my beauty advice, you've been reading for hours. Now what? Will you put the book down, buy a box of chocolates, and forget about the whole thing? Don't you dare! Maybe all these suggestions confuse you or discourage you, but I promise you that you'll soon—once you get the hang of it—be able to make beauty a part of your life, and a small part of it at that. You will be able to do each step of my beauty program more quickly than you can believe. Our models manage, and they are busier than anyone else I know. It's all a matter of attitude and habit.

Once you have assimilated the rules and made them work, you'll find that your beauty routine has become so much a part of your life that you will be completely unconscious of the many steps involved. But you will never grow unconscious of their exciting effects.

In summary, here's the easiest way to do it.

When you get out of bed in the morning, go to the window and take a dozen deep breaths. Breathe in slowly and let the air out slowly. Now exercise for five minutes (don't worry, those exercises are a lot easier than they seem). Then into the bathroom for your morning cleansing. Back to put on underwear and robe. Now, brush your hair for several minutes. Then apply your makeup. This should take about ten minutes after you've learned the techniques.

Now arrange your hair. A little cream on your hands. Put on your clean well-pressed dress, and take a look in the mirror. A pleasure, isn't it?

Whether you are at work or at home, take time during the day to stop at a window for more good deep breaths and try to find a few minutes to relax in complete solitude and quiet. Cream your hands after every washing.

Just before dinner, wash up and, if possible, take a bath. Restore your hairdo and freshen your makeup. If you're going out for the evening, take the time to start your makeup from scratch.

Before you go to bed, remove every trace of makeup. Go through the pamper plan step by step. Exercise for at least five minutes no matter what the hour. It will probably relax you and help you sleep. Do your beauty chores, such as manicuring. Brush your hair. Hop in bed.

Will this beauty program pay dividends? How well I know what it can do! It can make a model out of a teen-ager or a glowing sophisticate out of her mother. I have seen many a friend from high-school days wither and fade like a dried-up plant, and others swell like a blowfish.

199

Why? Because they haven't taken the time or trouble to protect themselves against the inroads of time. Why should you let that happen to you just because you won't devote time to yourself?

On the other hand, I have seen our models and my smart friends mature into their late forties and they are blooming, joyful pictures of what a woman can and should be. I've seen friends of my mother—all grandmothers—all alive and exciting women to this very day. You *can* control the forces of nature. You *can* keep your muscles firm and your skin alive. And if you do, you'll *live* every day of your life, rather than watch life pass you by. Take this book and make it your beauty bible. And be faithful to your own personal beauty program. Beauty in your life brings rewards beyond riches—serenity, confidence, admiration. These treasures are yours for the doing!

Photograph by Ormond Gigli

23
A Photographic Gallery
of the Top Models

In the following pages you will see, quite graphically, the growth and development of some of the most beautiful and successful girls in the world. They are from every walk of life and with many of the faults and attributes of women in less glamorous spheres. The difference is in what each girl has done with what she's got. . . .

Annami 51

Annmarie

ANNMARIE, 5'7", 33–23–35, is a tall, blue-eyed blond from Staten Island . . . she now lives in Manhattan and devotes her full time to modeling . . . she prefers classical music, tennis, swimming, and enjoys painting in watercolors . . . she also collects stamps and old pewter . . . a world traveler, she still elects New York City as her favorite place. . . .

NANCY BERG, 5'8", 34–24–34, a product of Wisconsin, is one of the most successful models because of her unique ability to portray both the glamourous sophisticate and the attractive, housewifely type . . . her background includes stints as a trick water-skier, and roles in summer stock, Broadway, film and television productions . . . skiing in Vermont and vacationing in Rome complete her usual year. . . .

Iris Bianchi

IRIS BIANCHI, 5'7½", 34–24–34, is one of the most-photographed high-fashion models of all time . . . born and raised in Italy, she now lives in New York City with her husband (an investment counselor) and their two children, Astrid and Edward . . . she avoids sports and politics in favor of ballet and opera . . . reading, oil painting, and cooking for her family fill most of her spare time. . . .

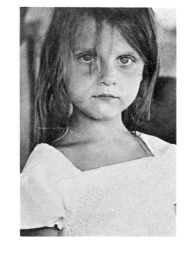

Martha Branch

MARTHA BRANCH, 5'8", 34–23–35, is a top junior model . . . her all-American good looks have graced many magazine covers and advertisements . . . an accomplished violinist, she also spends her very spare time painting . . . she's fond of musicals and good books and keeps trim by playing tennis regularly, swimming, and hiking . . . she and her stockbroker husband live in Manhattan. . . .

ABIGAIL BROWN, 5'10", 35–24–35, is an artist and a sculptress between fashion assignments . . . she majored in art and French at the University of Kansas, Beloit, N.Y.U. and the French Institute . . . her cultural preferences are classical and she admits little interest in sports . . . she is an avid reader and is especially pleased to write long, descriptive letters to family and friends. . . .

Helaine Carlin

HELAINE CARLIN, 5'7", 33–21–34, originally wanted to be a geometry teacher . . . she is now successful enough as a model to pursue courses in business and the stock market to guide her finances . . . she and her lawyer husband enjoy most of their off-hours with the ballet, and music by Brahms or Beethoven . . . art, films, and good books, along with bicycling, skiing, and golf complete their schedule . . . periodic trips to the gym help Helaine keep trim. . . .

Jane Cartwright

JANE CARTWRIGHT, 5'6½", 34–
25–35, is from Milton, Massa-
chusetts, and never dreamed of
being a model . . . a former art
student, she is now a part-time
water-colorist and has had several
"one woman" shows . . . Jane,
her TV announcer husband and
their three sons are outdoor en-
thusiasts, especially fond of water
sports and sailing . . . she finds
bicycling and a regular program of exercises keeps her in
shape. . . .

Melissa Congdon

MELISSA CONGDON, 5'8", 32–21–34, is from a family of six brothers and sisters . . . she's lived in several states, from California to New York, and now models out of London . . . a tall, slim, ash-blond, she's a prodigious writer . . . she owns a large collection of notebooks filled with her handwritten thoughts and remembrances . . . she also collects ancient tapestries and anything that looks like a lion. . . .

STEPHANI COOK, 5'8", 33–24–34, is an art history major from Barnard . . . when not modeling she and her husband enjoy Manhattan's fine offerings of ballet and drama . . . she collects lithographs and unusual antique toys and jewelry . . . without enough time to read as many good books as she'd like, she does devour the weekly New York Times Book Review . . . the RCAF exercises is her fitness ritual. . . .

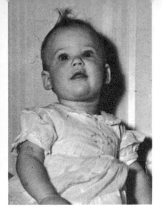

Colleen Corby

COLLEEN CORBY, 5'7", 32–23–33, *is one of the most popular teen models in the business . . . just answering her fan mail is now a large spare-time activity . . . movies, Broadway, and ballet are her favorite pastimes, when not bicycling or playing tennis . . . Colleen loves Italian food but balances this with regular "health nut" lunches to keep her youthful slim figure exactly right. . . .*

Agneta Darin

AGNETA DARIN, 5'7½", 32–23–34, is from Stockholm . . . she speaks several languages and is an outdoor type who prefers to spend her every free moment on horseback or swimming . . . she likes to read, see films, and collect antique porcelains and china, too . . . her husband, a top art director, is now giving her lessons in fine painting . . . he and Larry Rivers are her favorite artists. . . .

Joan Delaney

JOAN DELANEY, 5'8", 34-23-34, one of America's top junior models, was discovered in Woolworth's, where she worked after school . . . Paramount recently signed her for her first film, The President's Analyst . . . she loves to read, paint with watercolors, write prose, and collect glassware . . . she is also an accomplished dressmaker . . . Joan recently moved to Hollywood to pursue her new acting career. . . .

Rita Egan

RITA EGAN, 5'6", 33–21–34, originally planned to be a teacher but her part-time modeling while at St. John's University soon led to another career . . . now married and the mother of two children, she finds fun in such diversions as poker, skating, swimming, and photographing her family . . . her pet dislikes include pop art, avant-garde literature, and underground films. . . .

Paula Feiten

PAULA FEITEN, 5'7½", 32–23–35, *is one of today's most popular models . . . she, her film director husband and their little son, Jordan, live in a quaint apartment in the heart of old Greenwich Village with a pet named Greycat . . . Paula is an Aries and fascinated by astrology and such . . . she is also very fond of good books, classical music, her husband's films, and Italian food. . . .*

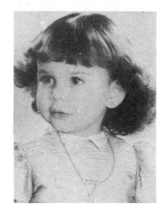

Norma Fidalgo (signature)

NORMA FIDALGO, 5'8", 35–24–35, is a Brazilian beauty . . . she is married to a photographer and they make their home on Manhattan's East Side . . . ballet by Nureyev, paintings by Chagall, and films by Fellini exemplify her cultural range . . . swimming, bicycling, and horseback riding are her favorite sports . . . she also likes to write long letters to friends back in Brazil, and prowl through antique shops. . . .

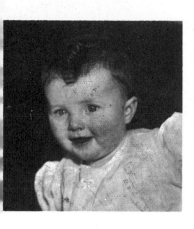
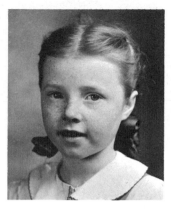

SHEILA FINN, 5'7½", 33–20–33, is that freckle-faced, red-haired, Irish gal . . . she is an expert baton twirler and one of the few models who've rated a Life cover . . . she is now married to Jerome Ducrot, a top photographer and film director . . . they live in New York's Gramercy Park with their little girl, Cecile . . . art and acting are Sheila's big interests, along with skiing and sailing for fun. . . .

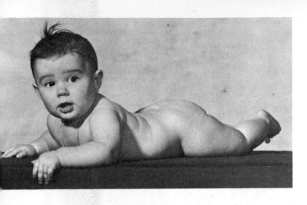

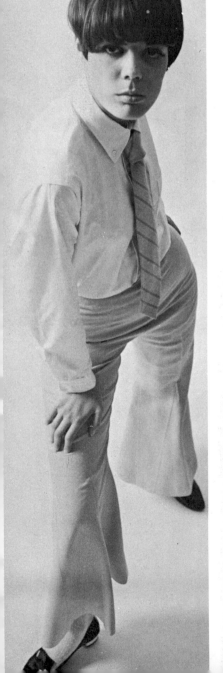

WALLIS FRANKEN, 5'7", 32–23–34, attended Briarcliff and decided on modeling as a career shortly after her first job . . . she's a vivacious and slim gal, quite visible in leading teen magazine layouts . . . her interests are wide-ranging, except for politics . . . theatre, films, popular music, painting, and photography fill her spare time . . . for sport and exercise its swimming and bicycling. . . .

AGNETA FRIEBERG, 5'9", 34–22–34, is a Swedish girl . . . her college studies and leisure interests center around art and psychology . . . the classics in music and literature and outdoor sports round out her activities . . . she doesn't much care for the big-party scene, preferring small, comfortable, informal gatherings . . . although she is well-traveled, New York's still her favorite city. . . .

MARILYN GRANO, 5'7", 33–22–34, is from Florida, and a former student of business administration at N.Y.U. . . . her quick success as a model cut short her academics and she now has time for only an occasional course or lecture . . . tennis, swimming, and water skiing are her sports . . . she's also fond of foreign films, ballet, opera, and good spy novels . . . otherwise her seven-year-old son provides enough intrigue, interest and exercise. . . .

Sunny Griffin

SUNNY GRIFFIN, 5'8", 33–23–35, is from Maryland, and a graduate of Hood College, where she majored in speech and drama . . . although she loathes baseball and football she is very much a sports-minded outdoor type . . . other interests include ballet, films, and theatre (her ambition is to be an actress) . . . her husband is in TV production and they make their home in Frenchtown, N.J. . . .

MARIA GUDY, 5'8½", 34–24–34, *is a cool beauty from the North of Iceland . . . she spends a part of every year there with her family . . . she speaks seven languages and is an accomplished sportswoman . . . European handball, horseback riding, and skiing are her favorites . . . she also paints, cooks, and sews . . . good films, historical novels, and vacations in Paris complete her typical year. . . .*

Rinske Hali

RINSKE HALI, 5'8", 34–24–34, is of Dutch descent . . . educated here, she still takes an occasional course in history, mythology, or anthropology . . . she enjoys all the cultural arts and all active sports—particularly swimming—but is a reluctant spectator . . . massages and bicycling are her fitness techniques . . . she and her husband live amidst Flemish/Dutch décor in New York City. . . .

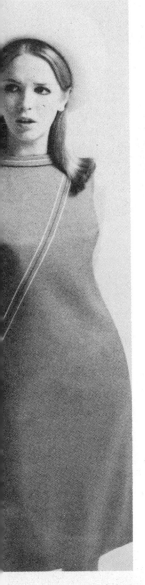

SUNNY HARNETT, 5'9½", 35–25–36, is one of the top all-time modeling greats . . . her sleek figure and ultra-chic features have been seen in hundreds of magazines and ads . . . she is now a fashion consultant for a large cosmetic firm . . . she and her husband, a recording executive, have a son, 11, and make their home in Manhattan . . . at one time Sunny's ambition was to be a commercial artist. . . .

GILLIAN HART, 5'8", 32–22–34, is a young mother who finds most of her spare-time activities are centered around her young son . . . she reports that her best exercise is gained in this manner, too . . . when free, historical novels, French films, classic guitar, and English antiques are her kind of diversion . . . her home and wardrobe reflect her ideas on the subjects of informality and comfort. . . .

DOLORES HAWKINS, 5'7", 33–22–35, should be recognized by all; she is easily one of the most successful models of all time . . . she's now married to a Manhattan realtor and they have a baby boy . . . when not held in New York by business most of their time is spent at their country home where Dolores indulges in her favorite pastime—horseback riding . . . when collecting antiques, its Early American for her. . . .

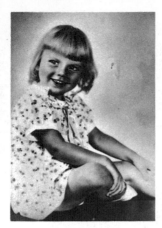

Heather Hewitt

HEATHER HEWITT, 5'9", 35–24–35, is one of the most versatile of models . . . from Vermont, she is a former Miss Boston University and Miss Vermont . . . she balances her fashion and TV assignments with a new acting and singing career . . . an expert skier and prize-winning artist, she finds both fitness and fun in the heated swimming pool she shares with her editor husband and daughter in Montclair, N.J. . . .

Cindy Hollingsworth

LUCINDA HOLLINGSWORTH, 5'9½", 33–23–36, is a native of Long Island and now lives in Manhattan with her husband, an investment counselor . . . a leading model whose face will be familiar to all, Lucinda prefers films, auctions, cooking, and card games for indoor doings . . . while outdoors it is likely to be skiing, skating, and sailing . . . pop art, politics, knitting, and best sellers hold the least interest for her. . . .

Pamela Huntington

PAMELA HUNTINGTON, 5'8½", 34–23–35, is from Los Angeles . . . she was educated at U.S.C. and the Los Angeles Conservatory of Music and had planned to pursue a career as a concert pianist . . . music is still a way of life for her, with her interests now ranging from Chopin to "The Turtles" . . . reading, painting, and writing poetry also please her . . . for exercise it is usually riding her horse or swimming. . . .

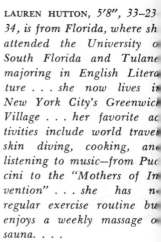

Lauren Hutton

LAUREN HUTTON, 5'8", 33–23–34, is from Florida, where she attended the University of South Florida and Tulane, majoring in English Literature . . . she now lives in New York City's Greenwich Village . . . her favorite activities include world travel, skin diving, cooking, and listening to music—from Puccini to the "Mothers of Invention" . . . she has no regular exercise routine but enjoys a weekly massage or sauna. . . .

Dorothea McGowan

DOROTHEA MCGOWAN, 5'8½", 33–23–34, *lives in Brooklyn . . . she has studied extensively in schools here and in Paris, her main interests being art, history, and biology . . . she's also adept at her native Irish dances and enjoys all sports—from skiing and riding to bird-watching and big game hunting . . . she keeps meticulous diaries of all her travels and can now be seen in her first film, the French production,* Who Are You, Polly Magoo? . . . .

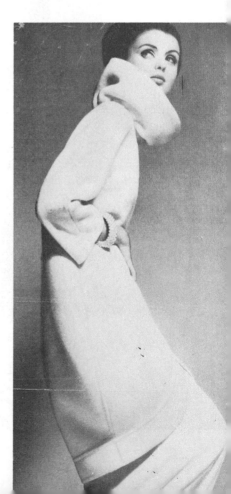

Kristen Topping

KIKI OLSEN (TOPPING), 5'7",
34–21–34, is a Danish import
. . . she and her executive
husband live on Long Island
and spend much of their free
time training their two Labra-
dors, skiing, fishing, or traveling . . . Kiki also finds time
for civic activities and knitting, needlepoint, gourmet
cooking, and collecting Meis-
sen porcelainware . . . massages, the Kounovsky exercises
and saunas keep her fit. . . .

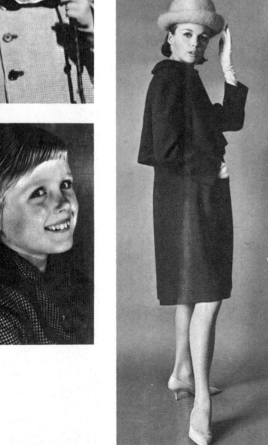

Suzy Parker (signature)

SUZY PARKER, 5'8½", 35–24–36, is undoubtedly the most famous name and face in modeling . . . she's also starred in several movies and TV shows in recent years . . . originally from Florida, she now lives in Los Angeles with her actor husband, Bradford Dillman . . . now "retired," she spends most of her time with her two daughters and an occasional good book . . . fine music, comfortable clothes, and home-cooked foods complete Suzy's fondnesses. . . .

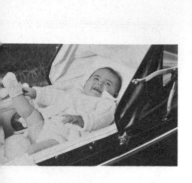

Catherine Pastrie

CATHERINE PASTRIE, 5'8", 33–23–33, *was born and educated in France . . . her favorite sport is skiing . . . she is a voracious reader and when not with a book she's likely to be knitting, antique hunting, playing with her young son, or traveling with her husband, also a model . . . her tastes in fashion, décor, and food are very French . . . she finds it easy to maintain her figure with little exercise. . . .*

Jean Patchett

JEAN PATCHETT, 5'9", 34–23–34, was the top model of the early 1950's . . . her beauty mark is one of the most famous . . . after a career of more than twelve years in front of the cameras she is now retired and makes her home in Manhattan with her husband, an investment broker, and two children . . . a graduate of Goucher College, her major studies were history and music . . . her sport (and exercise) is golf, whenever possible. . . .

Sondra R. Peterson

SONDRA PETERSON, 5'7", 33–22–34, *is from Kansas City, Missouri, and now spends most of her time in Paris, with occasional trips to New York . . . she originally planned to be a veterinarian . . . horseback riding and skiing are her favorite sports . . . in music she prefers jazz, in art it is the Surrealists, and in theatre it's comedy . . . she collects sixteenth- and seventeenth-century furniture and relics. . . .*

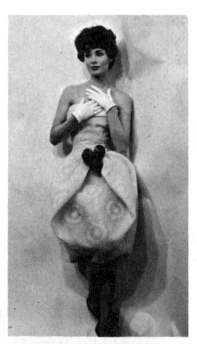

TERRY RENO, 5'8", 33–22–34, *a popular, young junior model, has already written her biography,* The Model, *published last year . . . from California, she now lives in Manhattan . . . her favorite sports are water-skiing, watching football, and playing a good game of gin . . . she also collects antiques and old watches . . . her ideas about food and fashion are decidedly French . . . she tries all the new exercise fads. . . .*

Cay Sanderson

CAY SANDERSON, 5'6", 33–22–33, from the Bronx, is a graduate of the University of Vermont where she majored in English and Art, and participated in a full range of extracurriculars, from yearbook editor to cheerleader . . . she is now married and lives in New York City with her husband, an adman . . . her sports and cultural interests are varied with preferences for horseback riding and skiing, painting in oils, and collecting antiques. . . .

Astrid Schiller

ASTRID SCHILLER, 5'8", 34–22–35, *was born and raised in Germany . . . her educational and cultural interests radiate from the worlds of art and ballet . . . a trained gymnast, she was about to embark on a career in physical education when she was discovered in Paris . . . she now spends much of her spare time skiing, swimming, riding, and traveling to visit her parents and friends in Frankfurt, Germany. . . .*

Beate Schulz

BEATE SCHULZ, 5'7", 34–22–34, was born in Germany and educated in German and British schools . . . she now lives in Manhattan with her husband, James Moore, a leading fashion photographer, and their young son . . . swimming and water skiing are her favorite sports, and she enjoys watching a good boxing match . . . she and her husband love to prepare Chinese and Italian gourmet meals together. . . .

JEAN SHRIMPTON, 5'9", 33–22–34, *took the fashion world by storm a short time ago . . . "The Shrimp" still maintains her top status and high fees . . . raised on a Buckinghamshire farm in Britain, a career in modeling was quite a surprise to her . . . now, just a matter of a few years later, and she's Number One, with a book written* The Truth About Modeling, *and a starring role in her first film,* Privilege. . . .

ISA STOPPI, 5'8½", 33–23–35, was born in Libya, Africa, and educated in Italy . . . music and art were her main interests until modeling became her career . . . her other activities now include Manhattan's many choices in theatre, film, ballet and discothèque . . . an athletic sort, she keeps fit with her favorite sport of fencing . . . collecting antique rings is her passionate hobby. . . .

Sara Thom

SARA THOM, 5'5½", 32–22–33, is the woman behind that exquisite, porcelain-fine face that is so familiar to magazine readers . . . now retired, she was one of the very top girls during her more than ten years as a model in the 1950's and 1960's . . . she was born in Little Rock, and attended the University of Arkansas, where she graduated cum laude and with a Phi Beta Kappa key . . . she and her family now live in Manhattan. . . .

Susan Van Wyck (signature)

SUSAN VAN WYCK, 5'6", 33–21–33, is a New Yorker who finds great exhilaration in living in Manhattan . . . she is very fond of the many films and plays, as well as the fun of trouping through the art galleries and antique shops . . . politics and cocktail parties hold little interest for her . . . swimming, skiing, and traveling abroad are the activities that she and her lawyer husband enjoy most. . . .

Marola Witt

MAROLA WITT, 5'7½", 33–22–34, was born in Berlin, Germany, during the last war . . . she was a thin, sickly child until she came to America at the age of fifteen . . . she was discovered at a dance by a fashion editor and soon discarded an art school scholarship for a new career in modeling . . . she is now married to a realtor and they live just outside of Manhattan with their two sons . . . swimming and skiing are the family sports. . . .

Jennifer Wood

JENNIFER WOOD, 5'8", 33–22–35, is one of the most athletic of models . . . as an infant, however, she nearly died of pneumonia and spent time in an incubator . . . swimming, skiing, tennis, and particularly horseback riding are her sports . . . Jennifer once owned a winning race horse and now has a thoroughbred hunter which she rides and shows regularly . . . travel, painting, and sculpting are her other pet interests. . . .

ACKNOWLEDGMENTS

The following names and picture credits indicate the models and the source of their photographs as they appear, from left to right, on the dust jacket.

Front flap: BEATE SCHULZ, by Francesco Scavullo; SUSAN VAN WYCK, courtesy, Country Set ©; SONDRA PETERSON, by Irving Penn; AGNETA DARIN, courtesy, Charles of the Ritz ©; LUCINDA HOLLINGSWORTH, courtesy, Monet ©. *Front cover:* TERRY RENO, courtesy, Sue Brett, Inc. ©; DOROTHEA McGOWAN, courtesy, DuPont ©; JEAN SHRIMPTON, courtesy, *Vogue* ©; HEATHER HEWITT, by Don Russell; ASTRID SCHILLER, n.a.; DOLORES HAWKINS, courtesy, Peter Pan ©; COLLEEN CORBY, courtesy, Peck & Peck ©; IRIS BIANCHI, courtesy, Christenfeld, Inc. ©. *Spine:* SUZY PARKER, courtesy, Dorothy O'Hara, Inc. ©. *Back cover:* RITA EGAN, by Roberta Booth; SARA THOM, by Jack Robinson; JEAN PATCHETT, courtesy, I. A. Wyner & Co. ©; STEPHANI COOK, by Simmons Jones; DIANE CONLON, by Susan Wilshire; BIRGITTA KLERCKER, n.a.; HEIDE WIEDECK, by Ron Harris. *Back flap:* SUNNY HARNETT, by William Helburn; MARTHA BRANCH, courtesy, Celanese, Arnel ©; SUNNY GRIFFIN, by Francesco Scavullo; PAULA FEITEN, by David McCabe; HELEN GERSTNER, n.a.

The following names and picture credits refer to the page by page layouts of the girls in the Photographic Gallery of the Top Models. The list is chronological (by age) in order, roughly arranged from top left to bottom right of each page, depending on the layout. Most of the baby photos, family snapshots and school portraits were provided by proud mothers or helpful sisters and for this the author and editors are most appreciative. Grateful thanks, too, to the many cooperative photographers, agents, models and scrapbook-keepers who lent us other hard-to-get pictures, proofs and tearsheets. In some cases it was not possible to obtain proper credit information by press time; these pictures are indicated as n.a., not available.

ANNMARIE: family/family/family/family/n.a./n.a./by Edward Hardin/by Garry Gross/ NANCY BERG: family/family/n.a./by Al Maley/by Jerrold Schatzberg/ IRIS BIANCHI: family/family/n.a./by Hiro/ courtesy, Eastern Air Lines/by Wilbur Pippin/ MARTHA BRANCH: by Jean La Valle/family/n.a./n.a./ courtesy, Seaton Hall/ ABIGAIL BROWN: family/family/family/family/n.a./by Frank X. Craig/n.a./ by Kublin/ HELAINE CARLIN: family/family/family/family/family/n.a./by Art Schiffer/ JANE CART-WRIGHT: family/n.a./n.a./by Robert L. Beckhard/by Robert L. Beckhard/STEPHANI COOK: family/ family/by Barnie/by Simmons Jones/by Simmons Jones/ MELISSA CONGDON: family/family/family/ family/family/n.a./n.a./ COLLEEN CORBY: family/family/family/n.a./n.a./by Richard Hochman/ AGNETA DARIN: family/family/family/family/by James Moore/by Francesco Scavullo/ JOAN DE-LANEY: family/family/family/by Shiffrin/n.a./courtesy, Paramount Pictures/ RITA EGAN: family/family/ family/family/n.a./n.a./n.a./ PAULA FEITEN: family/family/family/family/family/courtesy, Sue Brett, Inc./ NORMA FIDALGO: family/family/family/family/n.a./by Horn-Griner/n.a./ SHEILA FINN: family/ family/family/courtesy, Rose Marie Reid/n.a./ WALLIS FRANKEN: family/family/family/family/by J. Frederick Smith/by Justin Kerr/ AGNETA FRIEBERG: family/family/family/n.a./n.a./by Louis Faurer/ by Jerrold Schatzberg/ MARILYN GRANO: family/family/family/n.a./by Silano/courtesy, Simone Baron/ SUNNY GRIFFIN: family/by Howard Kenneth Jones/family/n.a./courtesy, *Glamour*/n.a./by William Helburn/ MARIA GUDY: family/family/n.a./n.a./n.a./n.a./ RINSKE HALI: family/family/family/ family/family/courtesy, Saks, Fifth Avenue/courtesy, DuPont/ SUNNY HARNETT: family/family/ family/n.a./by William Bell/by William Bell/by William Bell/n.a./ GILLIAN HART: family/family/ n.a./n.a./n.a./ DOLORES HAWKINS: family/family/by William Bell/by Richard Hochman/by Charles & Michael Fitzpatrick/n.a./ HEATHER HEWITT: family/family/family/by Lewis Brown/by Lee Kraft/by Pat Van Sant/by John Conboy/by Fred Pleasure/ LUCINDA HOLLINGSWORTH: family/family/ family/family/by Dick Dennis/courtesy, Balmain/courtesy, Monet/by Sherman Weisburd/ PAMELA HUNTINGTON: family/family/family/family/family/by John Foote/by Neal Barr/ LAUREN HUTTON: family/family/family/courtesy, Jorray Furs, Inc./courtesy, Main Street, Inc./courtesy, Dorothy Gray, Inc./ DOROTHEA McGOWAN: family/family/family/family/family/family/by Richard Avedon/n.a./ KIKI OLSEN: family/family/family/by Derby/n.a./n.a./ SUZY PARKER: family/family/family/by William Bell/ by William Bell/courtesy, Dorothy O'Hara, Inc./by Richard Avedon/ CATHERINE PASTRIE: family/ family/family/courtesy, Tricosa/n.a./n.a./ JEAN PATCHETT: family/family/family/by Lorstan/ courtesy, Max Factor & Co./by John Rawlings/by Irving Penn, © *Vogue*/ SONDRA PETERSON: family/ family/family/family/by H. Landshoff/n.a./n.a./by Irving Penn/ TERRY RENO: family/family/family/ family/family/by John Engstead/by Tony Ynocencio/ CAY SANDERSON: family/family/family/family/ family/family/n.a./n.a./ ASTRID SCHILLER: family/family/family/family/n.a./courtesy, Revlon/n.a./ BEATE SCHULZ: family/family/n.a./by Hubs Floter/by James Moore/n.a./ JEAN SHRIMPTON: family/family/family/by David Bailey, *Pix*/by Terry O'Neill, *Pix*/by David Montgomery, *Pix*/ ISA STOPPI: family/family/family/family/n.a./courtesy, Emba/n.a./ SARA THOM: family/family/family/ family/family/n.a./n.a./n.a./ SUSAN VAN WYCK: family/family/family/family/family/n.a./by Francesco Scavullo/n.a./ MAROLA WITT: family/family/family/family/by Will Weissberg/courtesy, Simplicity Patterns/ JENNIFER WOOD: family/family/family/family/by Lou Mitchell/n.a./n.a./

247

APPENDIX

Calorie Values in Common Foods*

248

The following tabulation of foods is arranged in separate lists, under fourteen subdivisions: milk, cheese, and eggs; meat, poultry, and fish; vegetables; dry beans and peas; fruits; grain products; macaroni, noodles, and rice; cereals; soups; fats, oils, and related products; sugars,

---

* According to the U.S. Department of Agriculture.

sweets, and related products; desserts; beverages (except for milk beverages and fruit juices) ; and miscellaneous.

Food items do not include added fat, sugar, sauce, or dressing unless such addition is specified in the listing.

Cup measure refers to a standard eight-ounce measuring cup, glass measure to an eight-ounce glass.

MILK, CHEESE, AND EGGS

		CALORIES
Fluid milk:		
Whole	1 cup or glass	160
Skim (fresh or nonfat dry reconstituted)	1 cup or glass	90
Buttermilk	1 cup or glass	90
Evaporated (undiluted)	½ cup	170
Condensed, sweetened (undiluted)	½ cup	490
Half-and-half (milk and cream)	1 cup	325
	1 tablespoon	20
Cream, light	1 tablespoon	30
Cream, heavy whipping	1 tablespoon	55
Yogurt (made from partially skimmed milk)	1 cup	120
Cheese:		
American Cheddar-type	1 ounce	115
	1-inch cube (⅗ ounce)	70
	½ cup grated (2 ounces)	225
Process American, Cheddar-type	1 ounce	105

249

		CALORIES
Blue-mold (or Roquefort-type)	1 ounce	105
Cottage, not creamed	2 tablespoons (1 ounce)	25
Cottage, creamed	2 tablespoons (1 ounce)	30
Cream	2 tablespoons (1 ounce)	105
Parmesan, dry, grated	2 tablespoons (⅓ ounce)	40
Swiss	1 ounce	105

Milk beverages:

Cocoa (all milk)	1 cup	235
Chocolate-flavored milk drink	1 cup	190
Malted milk	1 cup	280
Chocolate milkshake	One 12-ounce container	520
Ice cream soda, chocolate	1 large glass	455

Eggs:

Fried (including fat for frying)	1 large egg	100
Hard or soft cooked, "boiled"	1 large egg	80
Scrambled or omelet (including milk and fat for cooking)	1 large egg	110
Poached	1 large egg	80

MEAT, POULTRY, AND FISH

Beef, cooked, without bone: CALORIES

Pot roast or braised:

250

Lean and fat	3 ounces (1 thick or 2 thin slices, 4 by 2½ inches)	245
Lean only	2½ ounces (1 thick or 2 thin slices, 4 by 2 inches)	140

		CALORIES
Oven roast, cut having relatively large proportion of fat to lean:		
Lean and fat	3 ounces (1 thick or 2 thin slices, 4 by 2½ inches)	375
Lean only	2 ounces (1 thick or 2 thin slices, 4 by 1½ inches)	140
Oven roast, cut having relatively low proportion of fat to lean:		
Lean and fat	3 ounces (1 thick or 2 thin slices, 4 by 2½ inches)	165
Lean only	2½ ounces (1 thick or 2 thin slices, 4 by 2 inches)	115
Steak, broiled:		
Lean and fat	3 ounces (1 piece, 4 by 2½ inches by ½ inch)	330
Lean only	2 ounces (1 piece, 4 by 1½ inches by ½ inch)	115
Hamburger patty:		
Regular ground beef	3-ounce patty (about 4 patties per pound of raw meat)	245
Lean ground round	3-ounce patty (about 4 patties per pound of raw meat)	185
Corned beef, canned	3 ounces (1 piece, 4 by 2½ inches by ½ inch)	185
Corned beef hash, canned	3 ounces (scant half cup)	155
Dried beef, chipped	2 ounces (about ⅓ cup)	115
Meat loaf	2 ounces (1 piece, 4 by 2½ inches by ½ inch)	115

251

		CALORIES
Beef and vegetable stew	½ cup	105
Beef potpie, baked	1 pie, 4¼ inch diameter, about 8 ounces before baking	560
Chili con carne, canned:		
Without beans	½ cup	255
With beans	½ cup	170
Veal:		
Cutlet, broiled, meat only	3 ounces (1 piece, 4 by 2½ inches by ½ inch)	185
Lamb:		
Chop (about 2½ chops to a pound, as purchased) :		
Lean and fat	4 ounces	400
Lean only	2⅗ ounces	140
Roast leg:		
Lean and fat	3 ounces (1 thick or 2 thin slices, 3½ by 3 inches)	235
Lean only	2½ ounces (1 thick or 2 thin slices, 3½ by 2½ inches)	130
Pork, Fresh:		
Chop (about 3 chops to a pound, as purchased) :		
Lean and fat	2⅓ ounces	260
Lean only	2 ounces	155

252

Roast, loin:

Lean and fat	3 ounces (1 thick or 2 thin slices, 4 by 2½ inches)	310
Lean only	2⅖ ounces (1 thick or 2 thin slices, 3 by 2½ inches)	175

Pork, Cured:

Ham:

Lean and fat	3 ounces (1 thick or 2 thin slices, 4 by 2 inches)	245
Lean only	2⅕ ounces (1 thick or 2 thin slices, 3½ by 2 inches)	120
Bacon, broiled or fried	2 very thin slices	100

Sausage:

Bologna sausage	2 ounces (2 very thin slices, 4 inches in diameter)	170
Liver sausage (liverwurst)	2 ounces (4 very thin slices, 3 inches in diameter)	175
Vienna sausage, canned	2 ounces (4 to 5 sausages)	135
Pork sausage, bulk	2 ounces (1 patty, 2 inches in diameter), (4 to 5 patties per pound, raw)	270

Variety and luncheon meats:

Liver, beef, fried (includes fat for frying)	2 ounces (1 thick piece, 3 by 2½ inches)	130
Heart, beef, braised, trimmed of fat	3 ounces (1 thick piece, 4 by 2½ inches)	160
Tongue, beef, braised	3 ounces (1 thick slice, 4 by 2½ inches)	210
Frankfurter	1 frankfurter	155

253

Boiled ham	2 ounces (2 very thin slices, 3½ by 3½ inches)	135
Spiced ham, canned	2 ounces (2 thin slices, 3 by 2½ inches)	165
Chicken, cooked, without bone:		
Broiled	3 ounces (about ¼ of a small broiler)	185
Fried	½ breast (2⅘ ounces)	155
	1 leg (thigh and drumstick), 3 ounces	225
Canned	3½ ounces (½ cup)	200
Poultry pie (with potatoes, peas, and gravy)	1 small pie, 4¼ inches in diameter (about 8 ounces before cooking)	535
Fish and shellfish:		
Bluefish, baked	3 ounces (1 piece, 3½ by 2 inches by ½ inch)	135
Clams, shelled:		
Raw, meat only	3 ounces (about 4 medium clams)	65
Canned, clams and juice	3 ounces (1 scant half cup, 3 medium clams and juice)	45
Crab meat, canned or cooked	3 ounces, ½ cup	85
Fishsticks, breaded, cooked, frozen (including breading and fat for frying)	4 ounces (5 fishsticks)	200
Haddock, fried (including fat for frying)	3 ounces (1 fillet, 4 by 2½ inches by ½ inch)	140

254

		CALORIES
Mackerel:		
Broiled	3 ounces (1 piece, 4 by 3 inches by ½ inch)	200
Canned	3 ounces, solids and liquid (about ⅗ cup)	155
Ocean perch, fried (including egg, breadcrumbs, and fat for frying)	3 ounces (1 piece, 4 by 2½ inches by ½ inch)	195
Oysters, shucked: raw, meat only	½ cup (6 to 10 medium-size oysters, select)	80
Salmon:		
Broiled or baked	4 ounces (1 steak, 4½ by 2½ inches by ½ inch)	205
Canned (pink)	3 ounces, solids and liquid, about ⅗ cup	120
Sardines, canned in oil	3 ounces, drained solids (5 to 7 medium sardines)	175
Shrimp, canned, meat only	3 ounces (about 17 medium shrimp)	100
Tunafish, canned in oil, meat only	3 ounces (about ⅖ cup)	170

VEGETABLES

		CALORIES
Asparagus, cooked or canned	6 medium spears or ½ cup cut spears	20
Beans:		
Lima, green, cooked or canned	½ cup	80
Snap, green, wax or yellow, cooked or canned	½ cup	15

255

Beets, cooked or canned	½ cup, diced	30
Beet greens, cooked	½ cup	15
Broccoli, cooked	½ cup flower stalks	20
Brussels sprouts, cooked	½ cup	20
Cabbage:		
Raw	½ cup, shredded	10
	1 wedge, 3½ by 4½ inches	25
Coleslaw (with mayonnaise-type salad dressing)	½ cup	60
Cooked	½ cup	20
Carrots:		
Raw	1 carrot, 5½ inches by 1 inch in diameter, or 25 thin slices	20
	½ cup, grated	20
Cooked	½ cup, diced	20
Cauliflower, cooked	½ cup flower buds	10
Celery, raw	2 large stalks, 8 inches long, or 3 small stalks, 5 inches long	10
Chard, cooked	½ cup	15
Collards, cooked	½ cup	30
Corn:		
On cob, cooked	1 ear, 5 inches long	70
Kernels, cooked or canned	½ cup	85
Cress, garden, cooked	½ cup	20

		CALORIES
Cucumbers, raw, pared	6 slices, 1/8 inch thick, center section	5
Kale, cooked	1/2 cup	15
Kohlrabi, cooked	1/2 cup	20
Lettuce, raw	2 large or 4 small leaves	10
Mushrooms, canned	1/2 cup	20
Mustard greens, cooked	1/2 cup	20
Okra, cooked	4 pods, 3 inches long, 5/8 inch in diameter	10
Onions:		
Young, green, raw	6 small, without tops	20
Mature:		
Raw	1 onion, 2 1/2 inches in diameter	40
	1 tablespoon, chopped	5
Cooked	1/2 cup	30
Parsnips, cooked	1/2 cup	50
Peas, green:		
Cooked or canned	1/2 cup	60
Peppers, green:		
Raw or cooked	1 medium	10
Potatoes:		
Baked	1 medium, 2 1/2 inches in diameter (5 ounces raw)	90
Boiled	1/2 cup, diced	50
Chips (including fat for frying)	10 medium, 2 inches in diameter	115

French-fried (including fat for frying) :

Ready-to-eat	10 pieces, 2 inches by ½ inch by ½ inch	155
Frozen, heated, ready-to-serve	10 pieces, 2 inches by ½ inch by ½ inch	125
Hash-browned	½ cup	225

Mashed:

Milk added	½ cup	60
Milk and fat added	½ cup	90
Pan-fried, beginning with raw potatoes	½ cup	230
Radishes, raw	4 small	5
Sauerkraut, canned	½ cup	20
Spinach, cooked or canned	½ cup	20

Squash:

Summer, cooked	½ cup	15
Winter, baked, mashed	½ cup	65

Sweet potatoes:

Baked in jacket	1 medium, 5 by 2 inches (6 ounces raw)	155
Canned, vacuum or solid pack	½ cup	120

258 **Tomatoes:**

Raw	1 medium, 2 by 2½ inches (about ⅓ pound)	35
Cooked or canned	½ cup	25
Tomato juice, canned	½ cup	20

		CALORIES
Turnips, cooked	½ cup	20
Turnip greens, cooked	½ cup	15

DRY BEANS AND PEAS

		CALORIES
Red kidney beans, canned or cooked	½ cup, solids and liquid	115
Lima, cooked	½ cup, solids and liquid	130
Baked beans, with tomato or molasses:		
With pork	½ cup	160
Without pork	½ cup	155

FRUITS

		CALORIES
Apples, raw	1 medium, 2½ inches in diameter (about ⅓ pound)	70
Applejuice, canned	½ cup	60
Applesauce:		
Sweetened	½ cup	115
Unsweetened	½ cup	50
Apricots:		
Raw	3 (about 12 to a pound, as purchased)	55
Canned:		
Water pack	½ cup, halves and liquid	45
Heavy sirup pack	½ cup, halves and sirup	110

Dried, cooked, unsweetened	½ cup, fruit and juice	120
Frozen, sweetened	½ cup	125
Avocados:		
California varieties	½ of a 10-ounce avocado (3⅓ by 4¼ inches)	185
Florida varieties	½ of a 13-ounce avocado (4 by 3 inches)	160
Bananas, raw	1 banana (6 by 1½ inches, about ⅓ pound)	85
Berries:		
Blackberries, raw	½ cup	40
Blueberries, raw	½ cup	40
Raspberries:		
Fresh, red, raw	½ cup	35
Frozen, red, sweetened	½ cup	120
Fresh, black, raw	½ cup	50
Strawberries:		
Fresh, raw	½ cup	30
Frozen, sweetened	½ cup, sliced	140
Cantaloupe, raw	½ melon, 5 inches in diameter	60
Cherries:		
Raw:		
Sour	½ cup	30
Sweet	½ cup	40
Cranberry sauce, canned, sweetened	1 tablespoon	25

Cranberry juice cocktail, canned	½ cup	80
Dates, "fresh" and dried, pitted, cut	½ cup	245
Figs:		
Raw	3 small (1½ inches in diameter, about ¼ pound)	90
Canned, heavy sirup	½ cup	110
Dried	1 large (2 inches by 1 inch)	60
Fruit cocktail, canned in heavy sirup	½ cup	100
Grapefruit:		
Raw:		
White	½ medium (4¼ inches in diameter, No. 64's)	55
	½ cup sections	40
Pink or red	½ medium (4¼ inches in diameter, No. 64's)	60
Canned:		
Water pack	½ cup	35
Sirup pack	½ cup	90
Grapefruit juice:		
Fresh	½ cup	50
Canned:		
Unsweetened	½ cup	50
Sweetened	½ cup	65

261

Frozen, concentrate, diluted,
   ready-to-serve:

   Unsweetened | ½ cup | 50

   Sweetened | ½ cup | 60

Grapes, raw:

American-type (including Con-
   cord, Delaware, Niagara, and
   Scuppernong) , slip skin | 1 bunch (3½ by 3 inches;
   about 3½ ounces) | 45

½ cup, with skins and seeds | 30

European-type (including Malaga,
   Muscat, Thompson seedless,
   and Flame Tokay) , adherent
   skin | ½ cup | 50

Grapejuice, bottled | ½ cup | 80

Honeydew melon, raw | 1 wedge, 2 by 7 inches | 50

Lemon juice, raw or canned | ½ cup | 30

1 tablespoon | 5

**Lemonade, frozen concentrate,
sweetened, diluted, ready-to-
serve** | ½ cup | 55

Oranges, raw | 1 orange, 3 inches in diameter | 75

Orange juice:

Fresh | ½ cup | 55

Canned, unsweetened | ½ cup | 60

Frozen concentrate, diluted,
   ready-to-serve | ½ cup | 55

Peaches:

Raw	1 medium, 2 inches in diameter (about 1/4 pound)	35
	1/2 cup, sliced	30
Canned:		
Water pack	1/2 cup	40
Heavy sirup pack	1/2 cup	100
Dried, cooked, unsweetened	1/2 cup (5 to 6 halves and 3 tablespoons sirup)	110
Frozen, sweetened	1/2 cup	105

Pears:

Raw	1 pear, 3 by 2 1/2 inches in diameter	100
Canned in heavy sirup	1/2 cup	100

Pineapple:

Raw	1/2 cup, diced	40
Canned in heavy sirup:		
Crushed	1/2 cup	100
Sliced	2 small or 1 large slice and 2 tablespoons juice	90

Pineapple juice, canned   1/2 cup   70

Plums:

263

Raw	1 plum, 2 inches in diameter (about 2 ounces)	25
Canned, sirup pack	1/2 cup	100

Prunes, dried, cooked:

Unsweetened	½ cup (8 to 9 prunes and 2 tablespoons liquid)	150
Sweetened	½ cup (8 to 9 prunes and 2 tablespoons liquid)	255
Prune juice, canned	½ cup	100
Raisins, dried	½ cup	230
Rhubarb, cooked, sweetened	½ cup	190
Tangerine, raw	1 medium, 2½ inches in diameter (about ¼ pound)	40
Tangerine juice, canned	½ cup	50
Watermelon, raw	1 wedge, 4 by 8 inches long (about 2 pounds, including rind)	115

GRAIN PRODUCTS

Baking powder biscuit	1 biscuit, 2½ inches in diameter	140

Bread:

Cracked wheat	1 slice, ½ inch thick	60
Raisin	1 slice, ½ inch thick	60
Rye	1 slice, ½ inch thick	55
White	1 slice, ½ inch thick	60
Whole wheat	1 slice, ½ inch thick	55

		CALORIES
Corn grits, degermed, cooked	¾ cup	90
Crackers:		
Graham	4 small or 2 medium	55
Saltines	2 crackers, 2 inches square	35
Soda	2 crackers, 2½ inches square	50
Oyster	10 crackers	45
Doughnuts (cake type)	1 doughnut	125
Muffins:		
Plain	1 muffin, 2¾ inches in diameter	140
Bran	1 muffin, 2¾ inches in diameter	130
Corn	1 muffin, 2¾ inches in diameter	150
Pancakes (griddle cakes):		
Wheat (home recipe)	1 cake, 4 inches in diameter	60
Buckwheat (with buckwheat pancake mix)	1 cake, 4 inches in diameter	55
Rolls:		
Plain, pan	1 roll (16 ounces per dozen)	115
Hard, round	1 roll (22 ounces per dozen)	160
Sweet, pan	1 roll (18 ounces per dozen)	135
Rye wafers	2 wafers, 1⅞ by 3½ inches	45
Waffles	1 waffle, 4½ by 5½ inches by ½ inch	210

265

Wheat flours:

		CALORIES
Whole wheat	¾ cup, stirred	300
All-purpose (or family) flour	¾ cup, sifted	300
Wheat germ	¾ cup, stirred	185

MACARONI, NOODLES, AND RICE

		CALORIES
Macaroni, cooked	¾ cup	115
Macaroni and cheese	½ cup	235
Noodles, cooked	¾ cup	150
Rice, cooked	¾ cup	140
Spaghetti, cooked	¾ cup	115
Spaghetti with meat balls	¾ cup	250
Spaghetti in tomato sauce, with cheese	¾ cup	195

CEREALS

		CALORIES
Branflakes (40-percent bran)	1 ounce (about ⅘ cup)	85
Corn, puffed, pre-sweetened	1 ounce (about 1 cup)	110
Corn, shredded	1 ounce (about ⅘ cup)	110
Corn flakes	1 ounce (about 1⅓ cups)	110
Farina, cooked	¾ cup	75
Oat cereal (mixture mainly oat flour)	1 ounce (about 1⅛ cups)	115
Oatmeal or rolled oats, cooked	¾ cup	100
Rice flakes	1 cup (about 1 ounce)	115

266

		CALORIES
Rice, puffed	1 cup (about ½ ounce)	55
Wheat, puffed	1 ounce (about 2⅛ cups)	105
Presweetened	1 ounce (about 2⅛ cups)	105
Wheat, rolled, cooked	¾ cup	130
Wheat, shredded, plain (long, round, or bite-size)	1 ounce (1 large biscuit or about ½ cup bite-size)	100
Wheat flakes	1 ounce (about ¾ cup)	100

SOUPS

		CALORIES
Bean with pork	1 cup	170
Beef noodle	1 cup	70
Bouillon, broth, and consomme	1 cup	30
Chicken noodle	1 cup	65
Clam chowder	1 cup	85
Cream of asparagus	1 cup	155
Cream of mushroom	1 cup	135
Minestrone	1 cup	105
Oyster stew	1 cup (3 to 4 oysters)	200
Tomato	1 cup	90
Vegetable with beef broth	1 cup	80

FATS, OILS, AND RELATED PRODUCTS

		CALORIES
Butter or margarine	1 tablespoon	100
	1 pat or square (64 per pound)	50

Cooking fats:

Vegetable	1 tablespoon	110
Lard	1 tablespoon	125
Salad or cooking oils	1 tablespoon	125

Salad dressings:

French	1 tablespoon	60
Blue cheese, French	1 tablespoon	80
Home-cooked, boiled	1 tablespoon	30
Low-calorie	1 tablespoon	15
Mayonnaise	1 tablespoon	110
Salad dressing, commercial, plain (mayonnaise-type)	1 tablespoon	65
Thousand Island	1 tablespoon	75

SUGARS, SWEETS, AND RELATED PRODUCTS

CALORIES

Candy:

Caramels	1 ounce (3 medium caramels)	115
Chocolate creams	1 ounce (2 to 3 pieces, 35 to a pound)	125
Chocolate, milk, sweetened	1-ounce bar	150
Chocolate, milk, sweetened, with almonds	1-ounce bar	150
Chocolate mints	1 ounce (1 to 2 mints, 20 to a pound)	115

Fudge, milk chocolate, plain	1 ounce (1 piece, 1 to 1½ inches square)	115
Gumdrops	1 ounce (about 2½ large or 20 small)	100
Hard candy	1 ounce (3 to 4 candy balls, ¾ inch in diameter)	110
Jellybeans	1 ounce (10 beans)	105
Marshmallows	1 ounce (3 to 4 marshmallows, 60 to a pound)	90
Peanut brittle	1 ounce (1½ pieces, 2½ by 1¼ inches by ⅜ inch)	120

Sirup, honey, molasses:

Chocolate sirup	1 tablespoon	50
Honey, strained or extracted	1 tablespoon	65
Molasses, cane, light	1 tablespoon	50
Sirup, table blends	1 tablespoon	60
Jelly	1 tablespoon	55
Jam, marmalade, preserves	1 tablespoon	55
Sugar: White, granulated, or brown	1 teaspoon	15

DESSERTS

CALORIES

Apple betty	½ cup	170
Cakes:		
Angelcake	2-inch section (1/12 of 8-inch round cake)	110

269

Butter cakes:

Plain, without icing	1 piece, 3 by 2 by 1½ inches	200
	1 cupcake, 2¾ inches in diameter	145
Plain, with chocolate icing	2-inch sector ($\frac{1}{16}$ of 10-inch round layer cake)	370
	1 cupcake, 2¾ inches in diameter	185
Chocolate, with chocolate icing	2-inch sector ($\frac{1}{16}$ of 10-inch round layer cake)	445
Fruitcake, dark	1 piece, 2 by 2 inches by ½ inch	115
Gingerbread	1 piece, 2 by 2 inches	175
Pound cake	1 slice, 2¾ by 3 inches by ⅝ inch	140
Spongecake	2-inch sector ($\frac{1}{12}$ of 8-inch round cake)	120
Cookies, plain and assorted	1 cooky, 3 inches in diameter	120
Cornstarch pudding	½ cup	140
Custard, baked	½ cup	140
Figbars, small	1 figbar	55
Fruit ice	½ cup	75
Gelatin dessert, plain, ready-to-serve	½ cup	70
Ice cream, plain	1 container (3½ fluid ounces)	130

270

		CALORIES
Ice milk	½ cup (4 fluid ounces)	140

Pies:

Apple	4-inch sector (¼ of 9-inch pie)	345
Cherry	4-inch sector (¼ of 9-inch pie)	355
Custard	4-inch sector (¼ of 9-inch pie)	280
Lemon meringue	4-inch sector (¼ of 9-inch pie)	305
Mince	4-inch sector (¼ of 9-inch pie)	365
Pumpkin	4-inch sector (¼ of 9-inch pie)	275
Prune whip	½ cup	105
Rennet dessert pudding, ready-to-serve	½ cup	130
Sherbet	½ cup	130

BEVERAGES (NOT INCLUDING MILK AND FRUIT JUICES)

		CALORIES
Alcoholic beverages:		
Beer, 3.6 percent alcohol by weight	8-ounce glass	100
Whiskey, gin, rum:		
100-proof	1 jigger (1½ ounces)	125
90-proof	1 jigger (1½ ounces)	110
86-proof	1 jigger (1½ ounces)	105

		CALORIES
80-proof	1 jigger (1½ ounces)	100
70-proof	1 jigger (1½ ounces)	85
Wines:		
Table wines, such as Chablis, claret, Rhine wine, and sauterne)	1 wine glass (about 3 ounces)	75
Dessert wines (such as muscatel, port, sherry, and Tokay)	1 wine glass (about 3 ounces)	125
Carbonated beverages:		
Ginger ale	8-ounce glass	70
Cola-type	8-ounce glass	95
"Low-calorie" type beverage (with artificial sweetener)	8-ounce glass	10

MISCELLANEOUS

		CALORIES
Bouillon cube	1 cube, ⅝ inch	5
Nuts:		
Almonds, shelled	2 tablespoons (about 13 to 15 almonds)	105
Brazil nuts, shelled, broken pieces	2 tablespoons	115
Cashew nuts, roasted	2 tablespoons (about 4 to 5 nuts)	95
Coconut:		
Fresh, shredded meat	2 tablespoons	40
Dried, shredded, sweetened	2 tablespoons	45

		CALORIES
Peanuts, roasted, shelled	2 tablespoons	105
Peanut butter	1 tablespoon	95
Pecans, shelled halves	2 tablespoons (about 12 to 14 halves)	95
Walnuts, shelled:		
Black or native, chopped	2 tablespoons	100
English or Persian, halves	2 tablespoons (about 7 to 12 halves)	80
Olives:		
Green	4 medium or 3 extra large or 2 giant	15
Ripe	3 small or 2 large	15
Pickles, cucumber:		
Dill	1 large, 1¾ inches in diameter by 4 inches long	15
Sweet	1 pickle, ¾ inch in diameter by 2¾ inches long	30
Pizza (cheese)	5½-inch sector, ⅛ of a 14-inch pie	185
Popcorn, popped (with oil and salt added)	1 cup	65
Pretzels	5 small sticks	20
Relishes:		
Chili sauce	1 tablespoon	20
Tomato catsup	1 tablespoon	15

Gravy	2 tablespoons	35

Sauces:

White sauce, medium (1 cup milk, 2 tablespoons fat, and 2 tablespoons flour)	½ cup	215
Cheese sauce (medium white sauce with 2 tablespoons cheese per cup)	½ cup	245

Index